A CREATIVE STEP-BY-STEP GUIDE TO

GROWING
HERBS

A CREATIVE STEP-BY-STEP GUIDE TO

GROWING
HERBS

Authors
Yvonne Rees • Rosemary Titterington
Photographer
Neil Sutherland

WHITECAP BOOKS

This edition published 1995 by
Whitecap Books Ltd
351 Lynn Avenue
North Vancouver, B.C.
Canada V7J 2C4
CLB 3316
© 1994 CLB Publishing
Godalming, Surrey, England
Printed and bound in Singapore
ISBN 1-55110-155-6

Credits

Edited and designed: Ideas into Print
Photographs: Neil Sutherland
Photographic location: Iden Croft Herbs, Staplehurst, Kent
Typesetting: Ideas into Print and Ash Setting and Printing
Production Director: Gerald Hughes
Production: Ruth Arthur, Sally Connolly, Neil Randles

THE AUTHORS

Yvonne Rees has been involved with garden design and
maintenance, but in particular with the cultivation and use
of herbs, for over 20 years. For several years she worked in
London's Chelsea Physic Garden, one of the oldest
surviving collections of herbs and rare plants in the world.
Yvonne writes, lectures and broadcasts on all aspects of
garden design and gardening, but especially on herbs and
water gardens. She lives on the Welsh/English borders,
where she maintains an extensive herb garden designed for
her own culinary, household and medicinal use.

Rosemary Titterington was born into a 'herbal family' and
has been professionally involved in all aspects of herbs for
over 20 years. Recognition of her work on herbs was
rewarded by membership of the British Institute of
Horticulture in 1984. Her Kent nursery and gardens
display a wide range of herbs and contain the National
Mint and Origanum Collections. Rosemary is currently
engaged in lecturing, broadcasting on radio and TV, and
writing on all aspects of herbs, her main aim being to
encourage the use and enjoyment of these superb plants.

THE PHOTOGRAPHER

Neil Sutherland has more than 25 years experience in a
wide range of photographic fields, including still-life,
portraiture, reportage, natural history, cookery, landscape
and travel. His work has been published in countless books
and magazines throughout the world.

Half-title page: Borage flowers attract pollinating insects.
Title page: Herbal bags and polishes make ideal gifts.
Copyright page: Purple sage and hardy lungwort.

CONTENTS

Part One

GROWING HERBS

Herbs are fairly easy to please - after all, most of them grow vigorously in the wild and some may even be classed as wildflowers or weeds. You will find that the majority need little more than a sunny situation and a free-draining soil; most will not thrive in waterlogged ground at any rate. There are exceptions of course: herbs such as bogbean grow naturally beside ponds and streams, while woodland plants, such as woodruff, prefer shade; these will be useful for those difficult spots in the garden. It does pay to find out which conditions your herbs prefer and to accommodate them as closely as possible. That way, your plants are more likely to flourish and produce the healthiest, best-looking results. Another factor you will want to consider is the size of each plant, and herbs offer plenty of variety for tubs and borders alike. Some species, such as angelica and fennel, grow to well over 48in(120cm) tall, while others, including thyme and chamomile, are ground-huggers that produce a delightful carpet effect.

Herbs can be chosen for hedging - rosemary and santolina, for example, are ideal and can also be clipped into formal effects - or grown as an ornamental tree, such as bay, or as shrubs - juniper, myrtle and witch hazel are good examples. Then there is the wonderful range of colors to choose from: silver-leaved herbs, such as southernwood or santolina; the purple hues of fennels, sages and basils; the golden glow of marjoram and thyme; the bright reds, blues and yellows of bergamot, borage and marigold. Many herbs have attractive variegated foliage, too.

Left: A thyme seat makes a magnificent focal point in any garden.   *Right: A sprig of angelica.*

BAD PLANT

Avoid plants like this one, with large areas of bare stem and dead foliage. Weeds in the pot are also competing for precious nutrients.

GOOD PLANT

A healthy plant such as this has shape and vigor, with plenty of leaves right down to the base of the stem.

Choosing a good plant

To grow herbs successfully, it is important to start with a good, healthy plant and to plant it correctly. Always buy your plants from a good garden center or, better still, from a specialist nursery where you can obtain expert information and advice. Check the plants over thoroughly and avoid any that are limp and drooping, with sparse stems and just a few pale or discolored leaves. Look closely for any signs of disease or insect infestation and make sure that the soil has not dried out and shrunk away from the sides of the pot. If there is a mat of roots protruding from the base, this a sign that the plant is rootbound and should have been repotted long ago. Having chosen a healthy specimen, take it home carefully. Carry it upright at all times and protect it from the risk of pieces breaking off. Do not leave it in a hot, airless vehicle for any length of time. When you arrive home, take it outside straightaway and water it thoroughly before planting as soon as possible. Herbs are not difficult to grow; they are tolerant of most conditions and, being strongly flavored, they are not particularly attractive to slugs, snails and other pests. Given good conditions, you can achieve impressive results in a single season.

BAD PLANT

This plant has not been pinched out at the top, so has grown too long and leggy before keeling over.

GOOD PLANT

Choose this one in preference; it is compact and bushy, with a good shape.

BAD PLANT

Do not make the mistake of going for the larger plant because you think it is better value. This long, leggy plant may be in flower, but it has very little foliage on weak-looking stems and a mass of roots protruding from the base of the pot.

BAD PLANT

This stunted specimen has far too little foliage on its woody stems and a great deal of dead material.

GOOD PLANT

This good, compact little plant with a tight head of healthy foliage will grow quickly and well, once it is transplanted to the herb garden or patio container.

GOOD PLANT

By contrast, this specimen has a good shape, plenty of healthy-looking leaves around a central stem and a flower spike is beginning to form. Good-quality stock will ensure a successful garden or an impressive display, providing you continue to look after it correctly.

13

Herbs for sunny places

Few gardens have perfect soil and the ideal conditions for all the herbs you might wish to grow. Fortunately, there are plants that will flourish in a wide variety of soils and situations. Hot dry areas of the garden will suit many plants and you can help the soil to retain sufficient moisture by mulching it with a top dressing of potting mixture, gravel, bark or similar material. A garden that is full of sunshine and has plenty of moisture at root level will suit many herbs. Here we look at a range of herbs that will flourish in sunny areas of your garden.

Sun worshippers

The leaves of creeping and bushy varieties of thyme provide a variety of textures and patterns, especially when covered with dew or frost. There are many varieties of lavender, with flowers that range from pale blue to deep purple, white to deep pink. Dry, sunny gardens are ideal for the gray-leaved curry plant, with its bright yellow flowers and curry-like aroma. Use to garnish soups and egg dishes. The pretty members of the hyssop family develop flowers from midsummer onwards, attracting bees and butterflies. Rock hyssop has rich, blue, upright flowers. Other varieties have pink, blue, purple or white flowers. The larger hyssops tend to bend with the weight of flowers and look beautiful on raised beds and banks. Do not forget the marjoram family, the many purple, green and variegated sages, aromatic winter savory and rosemary - if you have space in your garden.

The sweet, spicy gray-green leaves of alecost, also known as costmary, may be used in stuffings and potpourri.

The long-lasting, pretty pink flowers of calamint are enhanced by bright green scented leaves.

The gray-green foliage of lavender always looks attractive, especially when smothered in flower spikes from summer onwards.

Few cats can resist the smell of catnip, a tall, gray-leaved plant with white flowers. Dry the leaves and stalks to make catnip mice.

Once established, most of the thyme family will cover a dry bank and provide color from spring until midsummer.

HERBS FOR DAMP, SUNNY PLACES

Damp sunbathers

Angelica needs damp soil to grow tender stalks for crystallizing. The leaves and stalks of this biennial plant are at their best in the first year. Coriander also thrives in sunny, damp locations. Because the plant bolts into flower, cut the leaves while young and pull out the plant when the 'carroty' leaves develop. The leaves of self heal form a useful ground cover mat. It has deep blue, 4in(10cm)- tall flowers. Bergamot, with its red, white, pink or purple flowers, is good for flavoring tea. Mace (Achillea declorans) has white flowerheads and leaves with a flavor reminiscent of the tropical spice of the same name.

Add small pieces of angelica leaf and stalk to fruit during cooking for a delicate fragrance and flavor.

Fresh carraway leaf is mild. For many centuries, the seeds were taken to relieve indigestion. Today they are used for flavoring many foods and pickles.

Remove the flowering heads of salad burnet to encourage tender new leaves for adding to salads.

In damp soil, comfrey produces abundant leaves for cropping and a profusion of beautiful flowers in a range of colors.

The strong, celery, yeasty flavor of lovage enhances many soups and stews, especially if they contain carrots. Use young leaves in salads.

Add young, tender rocket leaves to salads and eastern dishes. The pale cream flowers have a delicious mustard flavor.

Plant marsh mallow at the back of the border; it may grow to 6.5ft(2m) before the pale pink flowers open in late summer.

15

Herbs for shady places

Having a shady garden is no bar to growing a variety of herbs. Many prefer dappled shade and a well-drained soil, especially those with light or golden variegation on the leaves. Curly gold marjoram, golden marjoram, golden sage and variegated melissa (lemon balm) are good examples. All are excellent culinary herbs, but exposure to direct sunshine all day may spoil their appearance by browning the edges of the leaves. If you have an area of damp shade in your garden, the bright golden leaves of golden feverfew and golden meadowsweet, with its spires of fluffy white flowers in late spring, will provide bright splashes of color. Dry shade may seem to pose more of a problem, but do not despair; you can allow the pretty, variegated herb ground elder to take over! Periwinkles (*Vinca*) also flourish in dry shade. *V. major variegata* produces a bushy mass of leathery, evergreen leaves splashed with butter yellow that grow to 12in(30cm) or more high. The new growth in early spring is covered with sky blue flowers over many weeks. The lesser periwinkle varieties have silver-edged or gold-edged green leaves and blue flowers and provide useful ground cover, even in hostile situations. The humble ground ivy makes a pretty ground cover, with musky scented leaves and blue flowers.

*French sorrel
(Rumex acetosa)*

*Curly gold marjoram
(Origanum vulgare aureum
crispum)*

Below: *Golden feverfew retains its bright gold leaf color in the shade. Deadhead regularly to encourage fresh flowers to develop until the fall.*

Dappled shade

*The lemony acid leaves of French sorrel (*Rumex acetosa*) and buckler sorrel (*R. scutatus*) will be more tender when grown in shade. Bugle (*Ajuga reptans*) is a good ground cover when edging a shady border. Many varieties have beautifully colored leaves and rich blue flowers.
Golden feverfew produces a mass of bright green leaves and pretty white single or double flowers from spring to the fall. It has proved very helpful to migraine sufferers. Other herbs found at the edge of woodlands include primrose, wild strawberries, St. John's wort, foxgloves and valerian.*

*Bugle
(Ajuga reptans
'Burgundy Glow')*

16

HERBS FOR DAMP SHADE

Lady's mantle
(Alchemilla mollis)

*Golden
feverfew*
(Tanacetum
parthenium
aureum)

Ginger mint (Mentha x
gentilis 'Variegata')

Curled parsley
(Petroselinum
crispum)

Corsican mint
(Mentha requienii)

Pennyroyal
(Mentha pulegium)

Right: *Damp shade will encourage
ginger mint* (Mentha x gentilis
'Variegata') *to produce long red stems
carrying blue 'puffball' flowers
between the spicy green-and-gold
leaves. Cut regularly for new growth.*

Damp shade

*Curled and plain-leaved varieties
of parsley are slow to bolt into
flower in shade, but need rich,
moist soil to thrive. Creeping and
upright pennyroyal spreads into
a carpet of scented leaves along
paths and banks. Gingermint,
with its spicy green-and-gold leaf
variegation, has pale blue flowers
on upright stems from early
summer until the fall. Other
suitable herbs include flat-leaved
golden marjoram, sweet and dog
violets, celandine, centaury and
hedge hyssop.*

Herbs that thrive near water

Plants vary in their ability to live in really 'wet' soil. Many will flourish, but some may not survive if the water is stagnant, so it is far better if there is some flow of fresh water. There are various ways of improving the soil conditions: one solution is raising a bed so that the plants can send down taproots for water while leaving the rest of their roots in drained soil. Wet clay soil can be improved by installing proper drainage pipes and introducing plenty of grit and bulky natural compost. All these measures help to provide the air spaces in the soil that plants require in addition to water. Many beautiful herbs will thrive in damp, even marshy, situations, producing a succession of flowers in a wide range of colors.

A seaside garden will thrive if there are sheltering walls and hedges to provide protection from a strong prevailing wind, especially in winter. Overhead watering to wash off salt deposits helps plants to recover after stormy weather. Many people have created beautiful coastal gardens using herbs of all kinds - sheltered garden 'rooms' with their own microclimate.

The bright golden-yellow flowers of Elecampane (Inula helenium), which can grow up to 6.5ft(2m) high, are very dramatic in a large garden.

Meadowsweet (Filipendula), with its clouds of fluffy white flowers on slender stalks, has flat rosettes of green, gold or variegated green-gold leaves.

***Below:** Moist soil encourages sweet cicely to produce a mass of ferny, anise-scented leaves. Tiny white spots on the leaves are no cause for alarm - they are characteristic of the plant.*

Unimproved wild forms of comfrey (Symphytum) are usually found by water. Dwarf forms are available for small gardens.

Marsh mallow (Althaea officinalis) needs moist soil to produce edible tender young shoots and roots. The confection is made from the root extract.

HERBS FOR THE SEASIDE

Herbs with wet feet

For an interesting contrast of flower color and leaf shape, try planting purple loosestrife, with its upright foliage and flowers, spiky figwort, which has unusual tiny red-fringed flowers, and pink soapwort. Sweet cicely is pretty all year round, with its soft, ferny, aromatic leaves and white flowers, followed by large mahogany-colored seeds. In a large garden, self-supporting Joe Pye weed, or gravelroot, (Eupatorium purpureum) is a real talking point. A carefully planned seaside garden could enjoy a range of lavender flowers from early summer until late fall.

Evening primrose (Oenothera biennis) flourishes by the coast. The scented flowers open each night. Some improved varieties retain open flowers all day.

Bay (Laurus nobilis) enjoys salty air, but must be sheltered from cold winds.

The yellow to cream button flowers of cotton lavender (Santolina) would brighten any garden.

Aromatic, colorful sage makes good ground cover. Trim the tips of the shoots during the growing season so that plants remain bushy.

Thrift is a seaside plant often seen on clifftops. The pink flowers rise from flat cushions of leaves. There are many attractive cultivated varieties in several colors for the garden.

Rosemary (Rosmarinus officinalis) literally means 'dew of the sea'. It will flourish in a seaside atmosphere, providing it is warm and well sheltered from cold winds in winter.

Herbs for chalk and clay

Chalk is usually an easy soil to work with, but it does need plenty of humus to build up the nutrients and improve the water retention. In the case of heavy clay soils, it is a good idea to leave them weeded but 'rough' in the fall to allow frost to break down the clumps. Dig in rough, gritty compost when the soil is workable to improve the texture. Most herbs can be encouraged to grow in a range of unusual situations, but some really prefer a chalk soil. Red and green fennel, with their tall, feathery fronds and yellow flowers, provide plenty of leaves for cooking and are known to aid the digestion. Use the dried stalks to flavor fish and barbecue dishes. Borage also thrives on chalk, and the plants are usually humming with a wide variety of bees. Cut chives and garlic chives as new growth appears to provide delicious leaves and flowers for salads. The warm pink to deep purple flowers of marjoram seem more vibrant when the plant is growing on a chalk soil. All the origanum family are worth gathering and drying for winter use; there are many variations in flavor from sweet and mild to a biting pungent warmth.

Below: In spring, support the rapid, lush growth of comfrey. The flowers appear soon after and will be buzzing with bees.

Above: Be sure to plant horseradish in an area that it can safely colonize. It is pungent and delicious in sauces and the leaves are useful in 'bath bags' to ease aching joints after gardening.

Herbs that thrive in clay soil

Comfrey	Symphytum officinale
Elecampane	Inula helenium
Golden rod	Solidago virgaurea
Joe Pye weed	Eupatorium purpureum
Hemp agrimony	E. p. roseum
Horseradish	Armoracia rusticana
Jacob's ladder	Polemonium caeruleum
Tansy	Tanacetum vulgare

Fresh or dried, the firm stalks and flat golden flowerheads of tansy (here the curly variety) make it popular with flower arrangers.

Herbs for chalky soil

Most herbs prefer a neutral to alkaline soil, rather than an acid one, so it is worth experimenting with a range of herbs and mulching well. Suitable plants for chalky soil also include:

Pasque flower
Russian sage
Mullein
Juniper
Flax
Scabious
Dyer's chamomile
Toadflax
Wild wallflower

Left: In spring, the deep purple flowerbuds of chives open to a brighter purple and then fade to pale pink. The florets of young flowers add flavor and color to salads. Remove faded flowers to encourage new leaf growth and flowers. If left to ripen, gather the seeds when they become black and hard.

Chives (Allium schoenoprasum) *are attractive in groups or as an edging.*

The sky-blue flowers of borage (Borago officinalis) *provide plenty of edible flowers for drinks and salads.*

Oregano (Origanum vulgare) *develops a warm, pungent flavor to enhance Italian, French and Greek food.*

A garden would be incomplete without the useful evergreen leaves and pretty flowers of culinary thyme (Thymus vulgaris).

Compact marjoram (Origanum compactum)

Bronze fennel (Foeniculum vulgare purpurascens)

Creating a herb garden

Herbs are so versatile that half the fun of growing a collection is choosing and creating the garden or feature they are to make. If you just want a few culinary species within easy reach of the back door, you can grow a selection of herbs in containers or in a bed with various easy-to-grow vegetables to make a typical cottage-style kitchen garden. Other people want to grow as many species as they can find, in a semi-organized profusion of scents and colors. The informal herb garden may look slightly shaggy and a little bit wild, but in fact grows to quite a strict plan. This type of garden suits a large plot, but can be adapted to a small garden or even a single bed or border. If you prefer a formal style or are planning an ornamental garden feature, herbs are equally adaptable. Many of the shrubby types, such as rosemary, santolina, lavender and thyme, can be clipped into formal shapes and hedges, and the wonderful variety of leaf shapes and sizes among herbs makes them ideal as contrasting clumps of color planted in an intricate knot design or formal pattern. Herbs are an excellent choice, even for those who have little or no garden at all; you could plant up a miniature windowbox herb garden or arrange a few tubs in the tiniest backyard or on your high-rise balcony. The actual herbs you choose will be highly personal, too; you might treat them simply as ornamental and aromatic garden plants; select your favorite herbs for cooking; or perhaps make a selection of medicinal species or useful dye plants.

Above: A bold, formal design using creeping thyme plants in a regular wheel pattern. Use different herb plants within the segments to create a quickly made miniature herb garden.

Left: *Windowbox herb gardens are usually rather staid - just a selection of herbs standing neatly in a row. But this one is a wonderful profusion of edible herbs and fruits, with an excellent variety of shape and color.*

Right: *An informal herb garden where a splendid scented patchwork of plants almost smothers a winding path of stone stepping stones and completely disguises the garden's underlying, rectangular shape.*

Below: *A medieval-style knot garden can look really stunning. This wonderful pattern of different colored foliage plants forms the exquisite centerpiece of a small, but minutely planned, town garden.*

Summer maintenance

Herbs are generally easy to maintain, even in summer. Most aromatic herbs tolerate dry, sunny conditions and a poor, stony soil, while woodland herbs flourish in the kind of damp, shady positions many other garden plants abhor. Most herbs are rampant growers, spreading thick and fast during a single season, giving weeds no chance. Good ground cover means minimum watering, too. All but the moisture-loving herbs can survive with little or no watering, even in prolonged hot conditions. The only exception applies to herbs in containers, where the soil dries out more quickly. Here, regular watering is essential - but good drainage too, as herbs hate a waterlogged soil even more than a parched one. Patio and windowbox herbs will need regular feeding. Try to use an organic fertilizer, preferably a herbal feed, such as an infusion of nettles, yarrow, coltsfoot or comfrey. Heavily cropped garden herbs also benefit from an occasional feed during the growing season. Herbs do not really suffer much from insect attacks. An infusion of basil, elder or garlic with a spoonful of washing-up liquid or soft soap will deal with aphids; dried herbs, such as sage, can be sprinkled around plants to deter mildew, slugs and snails. Some shrubby herbs in formal herb gardens may need trimming during the summer.

Below: Add powdered fertilizers to the water or use a powdered herb, such as chamomile or sage, to protect seedlings and young plants from damping off.

Right: Tomato fertilizer is fine for herbs. You can also make up a strong infusion of garlic and dilute it with water to deter caterpillars, aphids and flea beetles from mature plants. Be sure to label all storage bottles clearly.

Left: *A mulch of small stones around young plants helps conserve moisture and deters weeds. Pull out weeds in spring while the herbs are establishing themselves and you should have no problems later on.*

Below: *Bark chips make an excellent mulch, as they are attractive to look at and eventually rot down to enrich the soil with valuable compost.*

Left: *Plant lush-growing herbs in close profusion and watering will become an infrequent chore. When watering, take the opportunity to add a herbal fertilizer, such as nettle or comfrey tea.*

Above: *Deadheading flowering herbs throughout the summer encourages new blooms. If the herbs are being grown to harvest the leaves, remove the flowerbuds before they open.*

25

Cutting back and tidying up

Like all vigorous perennial plants, herbs begin to look straggly or outgrow their allotted space at the end of each growing season. Even though you have been cropping plants for the kitchen or for drying, there will still be dead flowerheads to remove and diseased or damaged foliage to snip away. Older plants also tend to become woody or shapeless after a while. By cutting or pinching off dead or shriveled leaves, you also discourage disease and prevent a proliferation of slugs and snails. Cut back any dead or straggly stems almost to soil level. This may seem a little drastic, but will encourage stronger, more vigorous growth and a healthier plant. Trim small, mat-forming plants, such as thyme, with a pair of sharp kitchen scissors but use secateurs for taller, shrubby herbs, such as lavender, tansy and santolina, or even hedging shears for mature growth. In the informal garden, an annual cut-back and trim to remove unsightly stems and help plants to keep their shape, will suffice. The formal herb garden requires a little more thought and effort, particularly where a low hedging herb, such as box, lavender or rosemary, has been trimmed to create knot designs or geometric topiary shapes. Mulching between plants with colored pebbles or bark helps to maintain the desired shape of each herb. While plants are young and still being shaped, they may need trimming several times a year. To speed up the thickening process, prune out any strong woody branches growing horizontally from the main shape, trimming them back into the main canopy of the plant.

1 *In late summer, trim back the old flower stalks, top twigs and shoots of tall, shrubby plants, such as this Lavandula spica 'Munstead'.*

2 *Keep the plant outline slightly rounded in shape to help it shed heavy rain or snow during winter. Reduce the plant by two-thirds.*

3 *In spring, remove any winter-damaged twigs or branches to ensure a fine summer display of flowers on the neatened bushes.*

Left: *Encourage bushy growth of gray foliage on cotton lavender by cutting back all long, thin branches to a shoot just above the level of the mature wood in late winter or early spring. Keep the base wider than the top.*

Right: *Remove the dead flowers and untidy growth from bushy thymes in the fall. In spring, cut out dead and weak growth to encourage new shoots from healthy wood. Fill the center of the plant with a little fine potting mix to encourage rooting from the stems.*

Below: *Every year, remove excessive growth from rue to encourage the beautiful blue mound of leaves. Cut back to just above the mature wood where new shoots are visible. Wear gloves; rue may irritate sensitive skin.*

Below: *Every year, remove the top growth of tansy by cutting off the dead stalks close to the ground, just above any new, developing leaves. Do the same with fennel, French tarragon, lovage and woodruff.*

Only trim the tips of the branches on young sage plants. With older plants, you can cut off the top third to prevent them becoming straggly and shapeless.

Above: *All sages, including this purple sage, Salvia officinalis purpurescens, should be trimmed back in early spring to encourage plenty of new shoots with good leaf coloration.*

27

Propagating herbs by seed

1 *Small individual pots may be made of biodegradable fiber or reusable plastic. Fill them with a sterilized potting mix and water well.*

Growing herb plants from seed has several advantages: annual varieties can be replaced every year, there are considerable cost savings if you are planning, say, a hedge or lawn, and you will have access to a far wider variety of herb species and varieties. Most specialist herb seed stockists will mail supplies to their customers. The disadvantages are that, as with any plants grown from seed, you cannot guarantee that the new plants will be identical to the parent. Also, you may be left with many surplus plants, although you can usually sell or exchange these. The easiest way to sow seed is to sprinkle it directly onto the ground, preferably once the risk of frost is over. It helps if the soil is finely raked and free from weeds. A glass or plastic cloche over the seedbed protects young seedlings. Annual varieties with a long growing season are best started off indoors. This method is more reliable, as you can control the growing conditions, such as soil, temperature and light. You may even consider buying a purpose-made propagator to keep seeds ideally protected, ventilated and heated. To avoid the risk of 'damping off' - a condition in which young seedlings die off - use a sterilized potting mixture. White mold on the surface of the soil is a warning sign of this fungal infection. Watering with a weak infusion of chamomile can sometimes halt the condition before it progresses too far.

2 *Sprinkle a few seeds into each pot, using your fingertips for fine seeds. If the seeds are larger, press a couple of them lightly into the surface of the soil.*

3 *Arrange the pots in a propagating tray and top with a fine layer of vermiculite or sterilized potting mix, sprinkling it with your fingers to avoid making the layer too thick. Water lightly.*

Carefully label all pots and trays for future reference.

4 *Plant up larger trays in the same way, providing they have suitable drainage holes. Fill with about 1.6in (4cm) of sterilized seed potting mix, moisten well and sprinkle with seed.*

5 *Finish off with a fine layer of vermiculite or seed mix. Use an empty pot for better control over larger areas. Moisten with tepid water.*

6 *Cover the tray with paper, glass or a ventilated plastic cover. Leave it in a warm place or turn on the heat if the propagator is an electrically operated model.*

7 *Check the trays and pots every day or two and make sure the soil remains moist. Move them to a light situation as soon as the first seedlings appear.*

When the seedlings are large enough to handle, prick them out carefully into a deeper seed tray or peat pots.

29

Taking soft semi-ripe cuttings

1 *This bushy branch of red sage will provide plenty of material for cuttings. Examine it for signs of disease or pests and remove any thrips or whitefly by washing under running water. Select healthy, undamaged young branches.*

Many plants, including sage, marjoram, pineapple sage and lavender - in fact almost any herb that you wish to increase - will root well from cuttings taken at any time from late spring to early summer. Select healthy shoots at the right stage of growth, i.e. when the current season's shoots start to harden at the base. Test the shoot between your fingers. If it breaks, the shoot is either too soft or too hard. If it springs back when you let go, the shoot is at the right stage. On sage plants, as with many other herbs, the central growth on each branch is usually more advanced than the side shoots. Selecting this stem for propagation will encourage a bushy, attractive plant. If you are propagating from one of the colored sages (golden, purple or variegated), make certain that you select the shoot with the best coloration on the plant. In this way, you can be sure of maintaining good, well-colored plant stock. Remove any excess leaves on the stems, leaving about two leaves below the central leaf tips. If the cutting has too many leaves, it has to work to keep them firm with moisture. This can delay or prevent the more important task of forming roots for the new plant.

2 *Start by removing the lower leaves to expose the stem. Usually a gentle tug is all that is needed, but you can use a sharp knife for the task if necessary.*

3 *Remove all the leaves on the stem except for the tip leaf buds and the two leaves beneath. This will expose the soft new season's growth.*

4 *Cut through the stem at the point where the 'wood' is beginning to harden, just above the small stalks of the previous year's growth.*

5 *Make a hole with a dibble and insert the cuttings. These cuttings are being placed into pots, but a deep seed tray is just as suitable. Rooting in pots allows the cuttings plenty of room for root growth. Cuttings in trays will need to be potted on at an earlier stage, once rooting is established.*

Use a potting mixture with an open, gritty texture.

This dibble is custom-made, but the blunt end of a pen or pencil will serve equally well.

Propagating from soft woody cuttings

Rosemary, cotton lavenders, golden rod and many of the aromatic artemisias will root from soft, mature wood taken as cuttings during the summer and fall. Be adventurous and take cuttings from any plant, as long as it is free from disease and will not miss some of its growth. Strip the cutting of the lower leaves and cut the base at an angle to extend the area of soft bark, as this is where the roots will form. Insert the cutting into a tray or pot containing good-quality, open 'gritty' soil. Fine gravel, vermiculite and perlite are all suitable for cuttings. Work as quickly as possible; more cuttings die from delay, drying out and rough handling than from any other cause. Check the soil every day to make sure there is sufficient moisture, but do not overwater. Provide warmth at soil level if possible. Once rooted, all cuttings should be 'potted on' into individual pots with good-quality soil, as they will rapidly take up valuable nutrients.

The new season's soft stem growth appears as you remove the leaves.

2 Carefully pull the leaves from the shoot to expose the soft green stem. Leave the leading main shoot at the tip and two or three small groups of leaves below the leader.

1 Select healthy side branches with plenty of new growth. A gentle pull sideways will usually separate the shoot from the main stem.

3 Trim the cutting, making a clean cut across the young green stem. Keep the cut ends moist with a damp cloth if you have a lot of cuttings to prepare.

4 Insert the cutting until the lower leaves are almost touching the soil and firm it gently with the finger to ensure that no air pockets are left. The cutting should be upright and completely in contact with the soil.

Use a sharp knife to make a clean cut. Ragged ends may encourage rotting and disease.

If you are interrupted while planting cuttings and cannot finish immediately, place the cuttings in a sealed plastic bag and keep them overnight in the vegetable section of a refrigerator.

33

Taking tip cuttings from small plants

Small, shrubby plants, such as thyme, grow soft tips and stems from the woody, mature growth made during the previous season. These tips will root easily if taken between early summer and the onset of fall. Select a suitable bunch of soft growth from the garden plant and place it immediately in a plastic bag out of direct sunshine to prevent any loss of moisture from the leaves. Label each bag if you are taking cuttings from different plants, as it can be difficult to identify them later. The soil for cuttings must be gritty to provide plenty of spaces for air and water to percolate, and free-draining, to encourage rapid root growth. Rooting will take place in four to six weeks in a covered, heated propagator. It will be slower, but just as successful, if you support a plastic bag with three or more sticks or wire hoops over the tray. When new growth appears, ventilate the bag with a few holes, gradually increasing the number of holes over several days, before removing the bag completely.

2 Thoroughly water the tray about two hours before planting to allow excess water to drain away. Insert the cuttings 2in(5cm) apart in a tray or put 4-6 cuttings in a 4in(10cm) pot.

1 Trim pieces to 2-3in (5-7.5cm) by cutting through the semi-soft stem above a woody section. Remove the lower leaves.

Cut off young shoots with a sharp knife.

3 Always label the finished tray with the plant name and date, especially if you have taken plenty of cuttings. A final mist spray will refresh the leaves and also helps to 'settle' the soil.

Cuttings from different plants can share the same tray, as long as their aftercare is similar.

Rooted cuttings

After four weeks, the simple cuttings of thyme shown at the far lefthand side of the photograph have started to develop. The soil has been shaken off the cuttings on the righthand side to show the first fine roots. Most roots develop at the base, but a few may grow from the sides. When lifting rooted cuttings from the seed tray or pots, try to retain as much undisturbed soil as possible, as this encourages quick, healthy growth when the cuttings are potted on.

4 Cover the propagator with the lid, leaving the vents open. Put it in a warm place, such as under the staging of a greenhouse, but out of the sun.

35

Propagating herbs from root divisions

Many perennial herbs can be successfully propagated by dividing the roots to create new plants. The best time to do this is in the fall or early spring after the foliage has died down or withered. Root division is not only the simplest and cheapest way of acquiring new plants, it also regenerates the parent plant and prevents it growing too large. Providing the soil is not frozen or waterlogged, dig up the whole plant very carefully, using a couple of garden forks as a lever if the plant is big and well established. Lever the fork into the ground beside the plant and loosen the soil on all sides before attempting to lift it. Ease the soil from the roots, taking care not to damage them - washing with water can be a useful way to clean off dried or stubborn soil. Then gently tease the roots apart with your hands (protected with gloves if necessary) or use a garden fork and a sharp knife if the roots are tough or badly tangled.

Now is a good opportunity for you to check for any signs of disease or infestation, which you should cut away and burn before it spreads. After pulling apart the new, individual plants, lay them out, making sure that each section includes healthy roots and strong growth buds. Trim away any dead material and replant the new plants as soon as possible, at the same depth.

Another advantage of vegetative propagation, such as root division, is that it enables you to produce plants that are identical to the parent - something that cannot be guaranteed when growing from seed. This method is particularly suited to herbaceous plants with creeping roots and stems, such as mint, tansy and tarragon, and for herbs grown from bulbs, such as chives. With these, the clumps of tiny bulbils are easy to separate and replant at the correct depth.

1 This chive is about three years old and just starting into new leaf growth. This is a good time to lift and divide it into several new plants to replant into an attractive group or row.

Dividing large herb plants

Large herbs, such as comfrey, will often have developed large roots that break when you lift them. Discard any old wood - this is usually near the center of the plant - and trim off any large, broken or diseased roots to prevent them rotting in the ground. You can then begin to divide up the remaining segment into several smaller, more manageable pieces, each with its own strong root system and viable growth buds.

3 *Use your hands to tease the chives apart. They will divide naturally into small groups of bulbils that are easy to replant.*

Divide chive plants in the spring or fall.

Dividing French marjoram

Trim off hard stalks and old growth. Separate and break the clump into small plants, complete with roots. The roots and new growth are clustered around the base of the old stalks. Discard any old or very woody pieces.

A big clump of chives may require the leverage of two forks to break it apart.

2 *Divide the plant, using a fork if necessary, and loosen the soil around the roots. Clumps of chives will need dividing and transplanting every three or four years.*

Aromatic herbs

Since all herbs are naturally aromatic, to grow them is to create a scented garden automatically - heady with mingled scents on a sunny day as the heat of the sun releases all those essential oils, but even more wonderful after a quick summer shower. But if a fragrant garden or backyard is your primary intention, then you can select your plants specifically for their sweetness and compatibility of scent. Old-fashioned moss roses are an obvious starting point, the perfect companion for so many of the traditional cottage garden and herb plants, such as garden pinks, sweet william, stocks, lavenders and thymes. Plant bushy herbs, such as lavender, hyssop, bergamot and rosemary, in beds close to seating or paths where you will naturally brush against them. Keep marjorams, calamints, lemon balm, lemon verbena and chamomile in pots, tubs and raised beds where they are accessible. Creeping thymes and prostrate chamomiles are ideal underfoot; they will release their scents as they are trodden on. There are many bonuses to a scented garden: the wonderful range of shapes and colors, the beautiful flowers, and all the bees and butterflies they will attract.

Above: Spicy scented hyssop is one of the ingredients in eau-de-cologne. It has light green, narrow leaves and usually blue flowers, although this is a pretty pink variety. Attracts butterflies.

Left: Lemon balm, with its strong, fresh fragrance, is attractive in the bed or border. Harvest the leaves to make refreshing tisanes, a scented bath or add them to salads, sauces and fruits.

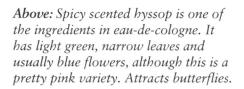

Right: Aromatic French marjoram makes a large clump of vigorous foliage, with pink buds and white flowers. It was once used to make small scented bags and toilet waters.

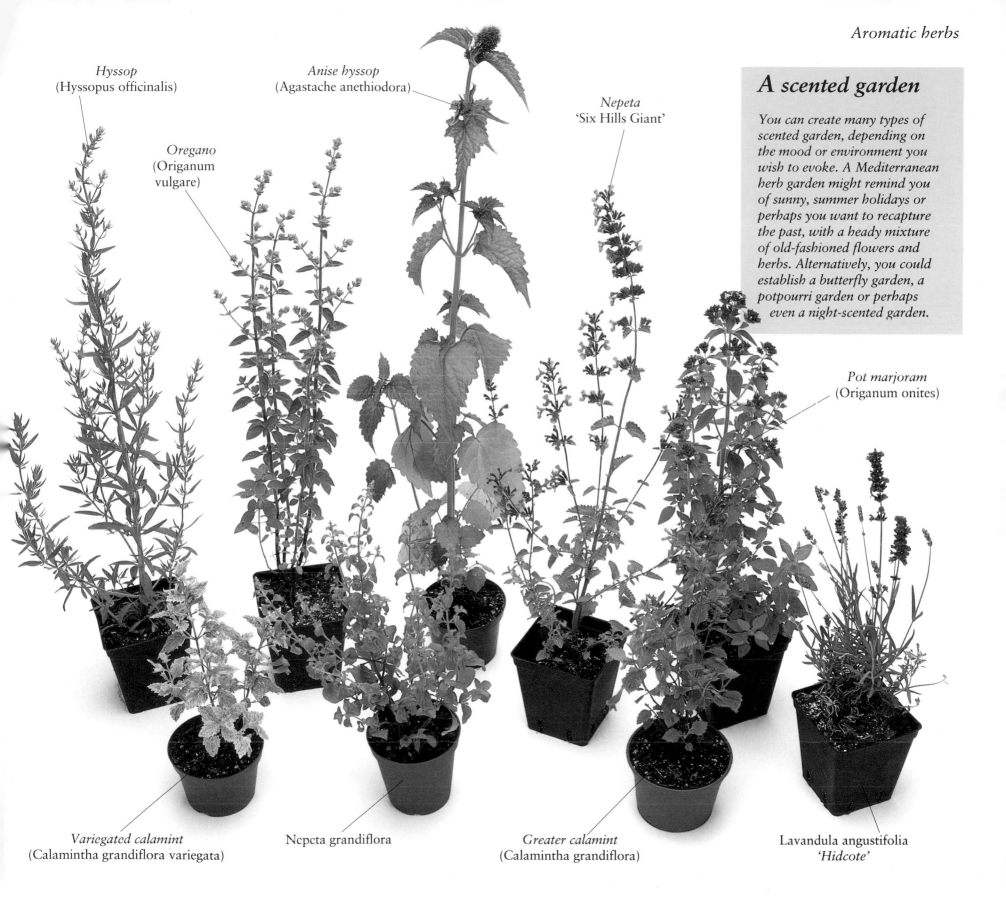

Hyssop
(Hyssopus officinalis)

Oregano
(Origanum
vulgare)

Anise hyssop
(Agastache anethiodora)

Nepeta
'Six Hills Giant'

A scented garden

You can create many types of scented garden, depending on the mood or environment you wish to evoke. A Mediterranean herb garden might remind you of sunny, summer holidays or perhaps you want to recapture the past, with a heady mixture of old-fashioned flowers and herbs. Alternatively, you could establish a butterfly garden, a potpourri garden or perhaps even a night-scented garden.

Pot marjoram
(Origanum onites)

Variegated calamint
(Calamintha grandiflora variegata)

Ncpcta grandiflora

Greater calamint
(Calamintha grandiflora)

Lavandula angustifolia
'Hidcote'

Herbs as ground cover

Good ground cover is the secret of any successful garden; prostrate plants tend to grow prolifically to create a dense carpet of foliage and sometimes make a mass of pretty flowers, too. These can be used to soften or link features, to cover ugly areas of bare soil and also to suppress any unwanted weeds, making them an excellent low-maintenance feature. In the herb garden, they are particularly effective. A scented carpet underfoot is especially attractive and the range of creeping herbal varieties available is wide for both sunny and shady positions that are so often a problem. Use herbs such as creeping thyme, *Thymus serpyllum*, savory, *Micromeria filiformis*, or chamomile to smother sunny paths and patio slabs with an aromatic carpet of foliage and flowers. They might soften the cracks or be allowed to spread and make a small scented lawn or raised seat. Do not forget their potential to clothe banks and the tops of walls, too. Shade-tolerant ground cover is always welcome for those difficult areas under shrubs or trees or by the side of the house, perhaps alongside a path or drive. The tiny mint, *Mentha requienii*, flourishes here, as do woodland herbs, such as pretty woodruff, *Galium odoratum*, with its low, spreading mass of starry white flowers; this is largely grown for its sweet scent, which intensifies when the herb is dried. Spotted lungwort, *Pulmonaria officinalis*, or ground ivy, *Glechoma hederacea*, could transform a dull area into a herbal delight.

Wall pepper
(Sedum acre)

Left: Purple sage and hardy lungwort, Pulmonaria. *The latter makes excellent ground cover in shade. Leaves and flowers appear in early spring, making it a good bee plant.*

Artemisia schmidtiana

Above: Herbs offer a wonderful variety of ground cover shape and color. These examples are useful in the dry, sunny conditions between patio slabs or beside paths.

Creeping lemon thyme
(Thymus serpyllum var.)

Right: Evergreen periwinkle makes excellent ground cover in shady areas, but flowers more freely in sun. Vinca major 'Variegata' *is a shrubby plant with cream-edged leaves.*

Roman wormwood
(Artemisia pontica)

Compact marjoram
(Marjoram compactum)

Above: Woodruff's advantage in the modern garden is that it thrives in damp, shady areas where few other plants will flourish. Loose sprays of white flowers appear in late spring.

Double-flowered chamomile
(Chamaemelum flore pleno)

Right: Donkey's ears, Stachys lanata, has large, soft, silver-gray foliage. This tough plant flourishes in almost any conditions, providing ground cover all year round.

Planting a chamomile lawn

Feathery foliaged chamomiles, with their pretty daisylike flowers, have been cultivated at least since the time of the Egyptians for their medicinal qualities, as a good dye plant (*Anthemis tinctoria*) and as excellent aromatic turfing material. The prostrate form is certainly one of the best plants for creating a small herbal lawn or turf seat. There are a many different species; the wild form, is generally called German chamomile, *Chamomilla recutita*, an annual that grows to about 39in(1m) high. This, together with the perennial, more mat-forming *Chamaemelum nobile*, are the types most favored for growing in gardens. One variety, *C. nobile* 'Treneague', has been specially developed for making herbal lawns, as it does not flower. It maintains a low, compact turf and there is no need to nip off the flowerheads to prevent the plants becoming straggly. A chamomile lawn needs a great deal of attention in the first year to prevent it being overcome by weeds, but once established, it will thrive from being trodden on and rolled in the growing season. *C. n.* 'Treneague' is propagated by division of the runners in spring or late summer. Other types can be sown in the fall or spring, but keep them well watered until the young plants are firmly established.

Although each plantlet is small, it should have a good, healthy root system.

3 *Continue dividing the plant into smaller plantlets, laying them gently in a row until you have the desired number.*

1 *Start by removing the chamomile plant from its pot or plastic wrapping and check the roots for any signs of damage or disease.*

2 *Hold the plant in two hands and pull gently at the rootball to divide the plant into two pieces. Carefully untangle the foliage where necessary.*

Chamaemelum nobile 'Treneague', a prostrate form, is ideal for lawns.

4 Transfer the new chamomile plants to a planting tray and sprinkle the roots with damp soil to keep them moist.

5 Take your tray of plantlets to the prepared and thoroughly weeded site and set them out 6in(15cm) apart.

Chamomile thrives on regular rolling or being trodden on. This variety grows to about 2in(5cm).

6 If kept well weeded and occasionally trimmed with shears, the chamomile will form a dense green sward, ideal for a small lawn or seat.

43

Thyme in patios and paving

Thyme is a most useful garden plant. Its tiny leaves and dense habit create a carpet, cushion or low hedge according to variety, and are ideal for softening harder landscaped features, such as walls, paths and the edges of containers. The most commonly seen species in the wild and in the garden is *Thymus vulgaris*, a shrubby perennial about 12in(30cm) high with tiny gray-green leaves and a mass of small white or mauve flowers. The creeping thyme, *Thymus serpyllum,* grows wild in Europe and can be planted among alpines in the rockery or in the cracks between the paving stones and slabs of a path or patio, where your feet will brush against the leaves, releasing a warm, pungent scent. The more upright varieties can be clipped into low, compact hedges, ideal for edging beds and borders or a formal herb garden design. There is a range of types and flavors to choose from, including gold and silver varieties such as 'Golden Lemon' and 'Silver Posie', which look lovely grown together in a thyme bed or contrasted with other herb shapes and colors. Lemon thyme, *Thymus x citriodorus,* is popular with cooks, ideal for adding to rich stews and stuffings. It has rounded green leaves and pale pink flowers and makes a compact, low mound of fresh, lemon-scented foliage.

Different varieties of thyme add color and interest to a bank in the garden.

Left: Thymus fragrantissimus *makes a dense dome of pale mauve flowers. Position it on a corner or close to a path to encourage the wonderfully fragrant scent to be released whenever anyone brushes past it.*

Growing thyme

Thyme can be propagated by seed, cuttings, layering or root division. To grow it from seed, sow it in early spring and plant out or thin to 10in(25cm) apart in well-drained soil. Thyme will thrive in any well-drained, sunny position and you should be able to crop it all year round, unless winter frosts are severe, in which case protect it with straw or soil. Harvest the leaves for drying just as the flower buds are opening by cutting the stems to about 2in(5cm) from the ground. Thyme is also an excellent bee plant.

1 To plant a creeping thyme beside a path or in between paving stones, first hollow out a planting pocket in the soil the right size for the plant.

2 Press the plant firmly into the soil, leaving no gaps around the rootball. All the foliage should remain on the surface and not be half-buried.

3 Label the thyme if you wish. It will soon spread. The many varieties include a lemon-scented and a gray-leaved, woolly form.

Thymus vulgaris is the most commonly grown species and often used in cooking.

Left: Different varieties of thyme make a dense carpet of tiny aromatic leaves and flowers, ideal for stony outcrops, steps, stone walls and rocky slopes. The patchwork of plants also helps to bind the thin soil together.

Right: A creeping variety of thyme is perfect for growing between patio slabs or alongside a path or stepping stones. It spreads and softens the edges of the stones and can survive being trodden on occasionally.

Rosemary for edging

It is said that where rosemary flourishes, a woman wears the trousers. In fact, it grows abundantly in the wild in Mediterranean countries and will do well in any sunny, sheltered site with a light, well-drained soil. In a northern climate, growing rosemary in a large, well-drained tub or container may be equally successful, providing the plant can be overwintered under glass. Given ideal conditions, rosemary will grow as high as 6.5ft(2m), and is a useful and decorative evergreen at the rear or center of herb or Mediterranean themed gardens. Its pungent, narrow leaves grow on woody stems, the dark green leaves have silvery undersides and the flowers, which cluster along spiked stems and appear from early spring to early summer, are many shades of blue, as well as pink and white. The plant is easy to propagate from seed or cuttings, layering or root division and needs very little attention to grow into a large, upright, rather shaggy shrub similar to lavender. However, it is also a good plant for trimming and shaping and may be grown as a hedge or formal edging plant around herb beds as an alternative to box, thyme or santolina. Place individual plants about 50cm(20in) apart and trim them immediately after they have flowered. Another alternative to growing rosemary as a focal point in a bed or border, is to train it against a sunny wall.

1 *To make a rosemary hedge, plant young plants of a similar size and the same variety every 20in(50cm). Or alternate rosemary with a contrasting plant, such as silver santolina.*

Below: To keep a rosemary bush in shape, trim it immediately after flowering. Snip off straggly younger stems at a natural break in the stem.

Dry or freeze cuttings

A distinctive flavor

A sprig of pungent rosemary, with its warm, distinctive flavor, is enough to enhance a joint of lamb, a pot of vegetable ratatouille or a barbecue marinade. Use sparingly, as it can turn bitter when taken in excess. Rosemary may be used to complement some desserts too: steep it in the white wine used to make syllabubs or flavor sugar for baking by adding a sprig to the jar.

Rosmarinus officinalis

Left: Rosemary makes a deep green, upright shrub, glossy with essential oils. It will grow as tall as 6.5ft(2m) in a sheltered position, such as against a sunny wall. The spiky leaves have a silvery hue and the stout stems become woody and gnarled with age.

2 *Place young plants into a light, well-drained soil, taking care not to damage stems or roots. Allow each plant to spread itself a little as it settles into its new position.*

3 *Continue planting. It is a good idea to clear away other plants from the immediate area so that the new ones can establish themselves. A little bark mulch keeps down weeds.*

Keep the soil at the same level as it was in the pot.

Keep the plants together for convenience and to make sure you have planted them all.

Above: *A rosemary hedge will establish itself within a couple of seasons. Keep it well trimmed, especially if you want a more formal look. Shape plants after flowering.*

4 *Water the plants in thoroughly to encourage the roots to spread out and make good growth. Use rainwater if possible or allow tapwater to stand so that the chlorine can evaporate. Chemicals may harm young plants.*

5 *Note the details of the herb on a garden tag. If you need to replace one of the plants or wish to extend the hedge in the future, you can then be sure of matching the existing plants.*

Tarragon - Mediterranean style

Tarragon, with its tall stems of narrow, bright green pointed leaves, has a wonderful, almost warm aniseed flavor that perfectly complements many dishes, from roast chicken to salad dressings and sauces for egg or fish. French tarragon is preferable, as it has a far superior flavor to the Russian variety and grows to about 39in(1m) high. The flowers are insignificant and rarely open fully in cooler climates, and the seed is not viable, so the plant must be propagated by cuttings or root division. Young plants should be planted out in late spring about 24in(60cm) apart in a sunny position. It is important that the soil is well drained and not too rich. This allows the roots plenty of space to spread, otherwise they will become waterlogged in winter and the plant may not survive. Its preference for a poor, free-draining soil and a sunny site makes tarragon an ideal candidate for a Mediterranean-style planting scheme. To protect the plant from frost in winter, it is a good idea to cut it right down and cover the roots with straw. Potting up a plant and bringing it into the greenhouse at the end of summer will maintain a supply of fresh leaves a little longer. Plants can also be lifted, divided into smaller sections and replanted; if you do this in the spring it will help preserve the flavor of the herb. Tarragon is best used fresh and stems can be cropped throughout the growing period.

3 *Remove the tarragon from its pot and lower it gently into the new container, taking care that the roots and stems are undisturbed.*

1 *Tarragon prefers a well-drained situation. If you plant it in a container, choose one that is made of a porous material, such as terracotta. Cover the drainage hole with pebbles or a crock.*

2 *Start filling the container with potting mixture - nothing too rich or the tarragon plant will overdo its root growth and take in too much moisture for the winter.*

4 Top up the container with potting mixture and firm it gently around the plant, making sure you have left no gaps or air pockets.

5 A sprinkling of gravel or pebbles on the surface of the soil will inhibit weeds and the development of mossy growth.

Harvest fresh leaves all summer.

6 Tarragon will grow to 24-36in (60-90cm) in a container. Unless the site is sheltered, bring the plant under cover for the winter or cut it down and cover the roots with straw.

Thymus drucei minus *with dwarf pinks.*

Bay (Laurus nobilis)

Nepeta 'Six Hills Giant'

Greek basil (Ocimum minimum *var.* Greek)

Sweet basil (Ocimum basilicum)

French tarragon (Artemisia dracunculus)

French marjoram (Origanum onites *x* 'French')

Creeping lemon thyme (T. serpyllum *var.*)

Left: *Here, tarragon is just one of the herbs included in a wonderful Mediterranean collection that would look marvelous in the corner of any garden or patio, providing it was sheltered and received plenty of sun.*

Planting up a parsley pot

Parsley is probably one of the most used herbs in the kitchen; a vital ingredient in stuffings, marinades and bouquet garnis, and invaluable as a garnish. However, it does not dry well, becoming virtually tasteless, so it is well worth growing it yourself to ensure a fresh supply. Parsley can be chopped and frozen for adding to soups, stews and marinades, but you can still eat it fresh throughout the winter by sowing seeds in the greenhouse in midsummer or potting up the roots of spring-grown plants to bring indoors. Cropping plants by the handful rather than the sprig can quickly outstrip supply if your garden is small. If space is limited, the answer might be multi-pocketed strawberry barrels, which suit parsley just as well and are perfect for backyards and patios. You can buy them in terracotta or plastic; alternatively, make your own from an old wooden barrel. A partly shady spot is ideal for parsley and be sure to provide plenty of moisture. Parsley is a biennial and the leaves taste best in the first year, becoming bitter and rather coarse in the second, so try to sow a fresh supply each year in spring and late summer. The seeds can take at least six weeks to germinate, but this can be speeded up by soaking them overnight in warm water and then soaking a fine tilth seed bed with boiling water before planting. Cover the seeds thinly with fine soil and thin the seedlings to about 10in(25cm) apart.

3 *Once you have released each plant by upturning and tapping the pot, you may need to squeeze the rootball slightly to make it fit through the holes in the parsley pot. Avoid damaging the roots.*

Support the plant gently in your hand as you make it ready for planting.

The dense foliage of curled parsley (Petroselinum crispum) looks best in this kind of container.

1 *Place a few crocks or broken pieces of china in the bottom of the pot to ensure that the drainage holes do not become blocked.*

2 *Fill the pot with potting mix until you nearly reach the level of the planting spaces - in taller pots, these might appear at various heights.*

4 Insert the parsley plants into the planting holes, pressing them firmly into the potting mixture. Make sure that the rootball is covered and the plants are the right way up.

5 Place the final plant in the top of the container, making sure that it is planted at the correct height to grow right out of the top.

6 After filling and firming with potting mixture, sprinkle a handful of small stones or gravel on the surface to reduce moisture loss.

Parsley seeds or seedlings are both suitable for planting.

7 The finished pot provides plenty of parsley for picking within a very small planted area. Pinch off flower stalks as they appear to maintain good growth.

51

The versatility of mint

Members of the mint family are available in a wonderful variety of types and scents, but many people are afraid to grow them on account of their vigorous habit, which they fear might swamp neighboring plants. If this is a worry in your garden, you might position your mints in tubs or containers or even grow a whole range of types in a raised mint bed, where the creeping rhizomes will be contained. If you do want to plant out mint in the main garden, try restraining it by planting it in a pot or bucket before burying the container in the soil. In all cases, remember to feed and water carefully. Moving plants every few years is a good idea to avoid a build-up of disease. Most mints will enjoy some shade, and the creeping varieties make good carpet plants. It is best not to propagate mints from seed as they hybridize easily, but 6in(15cm) pieces of stem should root easily if laid horizontally about 2in(5cm) deep in moist soil in the spring. Plants will die down in winter and roots may need protecting with straw in cold areas. Fork manure compost into the bed in the fall, chopping the runners a few times with your spade to encourage good new growth the following spring. Transfer a few runners to a box of rich potting mix in a heated greenhouse for winter use.

The curled spearmint has unusual, deeply veined leaves.

Spearmint (Mentha spicata) is the most common mint.

The Corsican mint (Mentha requienii) makes a dense carpet of miniature leaves and flowers.

Black spearmint has bold purple stems and purple-tinged leaves.

Lemon mint has a fresh lemon scent, which is useful for cooking and also in cosmetics.

The buddleia mint has an upright habit and attractive soft, green foliage.

Spicy ginger mint (M. x gentilis 'Variegata') has pretty green foliage.

The pennyroyal (Mentha pulegium) prefers a damp, shady spot.

Creeping forms of pennyroyal make a wonderful scented carpet of small leaves.

Red raripila (M. raripila rubra) has a spearmint flavor.

Peppermint (M. x piperita) has a refreshing mint flavor and antiseptic properties.

Bowles apple mint has unusual thick, gray, feltlike leaves and a fresh apple scent.

Above: *An ingenious way of growing a whole collection of mints is to plant them in a variety of terracotta pots of different sizes, thus displaying their range of color, shape and texture.*

Chives - with a hint of onion

You can grow chives from seed or you can buy them from herb stockists. However, being a member of the onion family, perennial chives are usually propagated by dividing the bulbs and you should do this every three years in any case to regenerate the plants. Simply dig up a clump carefully and gently prize the bulbs apart before planting them out in small groups of four or five. The soil must be rich and damp, but chives are not too fussy about sun or shade. Sometimes the spiky, green, hollow leaves begin to look a little yellow and this means the soil has become too impoverished or possibly too dry. Enriching the soil with good-quality potting mixture or more conscientious watering is the answer, especially if the chives are grown in a tub or other type of container. Their spiky shape can make an effective contrast against other, leafier herbs and yet they only grow about 12in(30cm) tall, which makes them a good choice where space is limited. Snip the leaves with a knife or scissors throughout the summer to provide an interesting green garnish and a mild onion flavor to virtually any savory dish. The flowers appear in early summer - fluffy mauve pompons on the top of strong, hollow stalks. It is a good idea to nip these off despite their attractive appearance, to encourage good leaf growth.

Giant chives (Allium schoenoprasum sibiricum)

Chives (Allium schoenoprasum) *the smallest of the onion family.*

Allium perutile, *the everlasting onion.*

Right: *Children might enjoy growing chives in a novelty pot or container, usually made of terracotta, where the spikes and flowers make a focal point.*

Below: *All the alliums can profitably take their place in the herb garden beside chives. All feature that mild onion flavor in the long hollow stems, so useful for adding to sauces, salads, marinades and garnishes, although the larger types may have a coarser taste and texture. Each has its own particular use: tree onion bulbs make good spring onions (scallions); hardy Welsh onions remain green throughout winter.*

Right: *Garlic chives in a pot make a decorative spiky plant. Their mild garlic flavor makes them perfect for adding to dishes where a more delicate garlic taste is preferred.*

Tree, or Egyptian, onion
(Allium cepa *var.* proliferum)

Welsh onion, or ciboule
(Allium fistulosum)

Traditional role

Chives were traditionally a useful cottage garden plant, as well as a tasty herb for the table. They were believed to discourage carrot fly if grown near to carrots; to prevent fruit scab in the orchard; cure black spot on roses and mildew in gooseberries. Medicinally, chives are supposed to be good for the digestion.

Chives are the most delicately flavored member of the Allium *family*. The flowers are delicious in salads.

Feathery dill and fennel

Dill and fennel cannot be grown near each other as they will cross fertilize, so unless your garden is a large one, you will have to choose between them. Both have wonderful feathery foliage that looks magnificent wherever it is planted, whether as a focal point in the herb garden or as part of a more general scheme, and it contrasts strongly with other, fleshier foliage. Neither plant dries well in the leaf, but the seeds will retain a good, warm flavor with useful sedative effects. You can use these in baking or infuse them in boiling water to make a good digestive tea or effective eyewash. Used fresh, dill leaves have a subtle aniseed aroma, perfect with fish and roast meats, while sprigs make a lovely garnish. Fennel has a much stronger flavor. Dill is a hardy annual that needs a sunny, sheltered spot. It does not transplant well, so it is a good idea to sow seeds in situ and then thin these out to about 8in(20cm) apart. Sow dill in spring if you want the seeds or at any time between spring and midsummer if you prefer to use the leaves. Fennel is a more robust perennial, reaching over 5ft(1.5m) tall and producing large umbels of yellow flowers in midsummer. There are several varieties, including a superb bronze form. The swollen base of the annual Florence fennel is used as a celerylike vegetable. Fennel can be propagated by seed in spring - thin the seedlings to 20in(50cm) apart - or by root division in the fall. Growing several plants means you can use some for their leaves and others for seed. Collect the seedheads as the seeds change color and hang them in a well-aired place to dry, with a cloth or paper bag below to catch the seeds.

1 *When the dill plant is just 4-6in (12-15cm) tall, the foliage will be very soft and tender; trim off what you need with a pair of sharp scissors.*

2 *The soft feathery leaves will have a strong, pungent flavor and are ideal for chopping into salads and egg dishes. They also make an attractive garnish for young vegetables.*

3 *When cropping herbs for culinary use, always cut the sprigs above the point where the new leaves are developing in order to encourage the development of new growth.*

Health and beauty

To make a soothing eyewash, mix one teaspoonful of fennel seeds with one of the sweetish aromatic herbs, such as roses or celandine, and about ¾ pint(400ml) of boiling water. Strain and cool before using. Make fresh each time. Fennel is popular as an ingredient in beauty products, including hair rinse (steep about 10oz/28gm of dried fennel in 1pt/550ml of boiling water and cool); it is used as a skin softener (fennel extract combined with yogurt and honey) and in toning lotions with elderflowers.

Above: Red fennel is an eye-catching, vigorous plant with a strong aniseed flavor. In cooking, it is the perfect partner for oily fish and aids digestion.

Above: Green fennel is a splendid architectural plant, tall and elegantly feathery in the herb bed or herbaceous border.

4 Once the dill has reached this size, it has become slightly coarser and a more robust kind of herb, perfect for adding to or garnishing fish dishes, such as pickled or poached salmon.

5 The mature dill plant, with its sturdy stem and flowers not quite out of bud, is used in pickles and chutneys. Its warm, spicy flavor counteracts the acidity of the vinegar.

6 Once the flowers are fully out on dill, the herb does not have such a good flavor and the texture is rather woody. It is still a useful plant for flower arranging.

57

Basil - a Mediterranean taste

An aromatic native of India, basil is well worth growing as an annual in cooler climates for its wonderful flavor; dried, it has a completely different taste. Basil is too tender for the general herb garden, but it may do well during the summer on a sunny, well sheltered patio with other tub-grown herbs. You could grow it under glass in a south-facing, protected corner of the garden or in the greenhouse with plenty of rich compost among the sweet peppers, eggplants and tomatoes. Regular watering and pinching out the top shoots are essential for good bushy growth. Basil is usually grown from seed in early spring to give as long a growing season as possible. Sow the seeds indoors or in a heated greenhouse and keep the potting mixture well watered. Once they are big enough, transplant the seedlings into individual pots or boxes for growing indoors or in the greenhouse. The soil should be well drained but moist, rich yet not heavy. Harvest continually during the growing season by cutting back the top and side shoots to the second pair of leaves. Left to its own devices, basil produces long spikes of white or purplish flowers from midsummer onwards.

1 *Pinching out the top growth of basil is essential if you wish to create a well-shaped, bushy plant. This is best done with the fingertips.*

Piquant pesto

Basil is perfect with tomatoes and most hearty savory dishes. Try chopping and steeping the leaves in oil or vinegar as a flavoring. Make pesto sauce by pounding fresh basil leaves to a pulp and mixing them with garlic, olive oil, parmesan cheese and ground pine kernels or walnuts. Use in pastas, soups or herb and garlic bread.

Below: Basil is available in a surprising variety of types and colors, from tiny-leaved Greek basil to purple forms with large crinkly leaves.

Bush basil
(Ocimum minimum)

Sweet basil
(Ocimum basilicum)

Red/purple ruffles basil
(Ocimum basilicum 'Red Ruffles')

Greek basil
(Ocimum minimum Greek variety)

Bush basil
(Ocimum minimum)

Dark opal basil
(Ocimum basilicum purpurea)

2 *If you pinch the stem sharply between the finger and thumb, the top set of leaves should come away cleanly and easily.*

Sweet basil (Ocimum basilicum) ready for trimming.

3 *The trimmed plant will subsequently grow from the sides to produce a well-shaped, more compact specimen. Harvest the leaves while they are still young.*

Sweet basil grows well in pots, both indoors and outside.

Sweet basil (Ocimum basilicum)

Cinnamon basil (Ocimum basilicum 'Cinnamon')

Anise basil (Ocimum basilicum Anise)

Ocimum basilicum, 'Red Ruffles'

Ocimum basilicum 'Green Ruffles'

Santolina as a hedge

Santolina, or cotton lavender as it is commonly known, is a most attractive garden plant, as well as a useful and aromatic household herb. It prefers a light, dry soil and a sunny position, where it will make a mound of tiny, feathery, gray leaves about 24in(60cm) high, topped with a mass of long stalks and little yellow or pale cream button flowers in midsummer. It looks fabulous when planted with other herbs and plants that have blue, gray or silver leaves and soft, downy foliage. Alternatively, use it to lighten up the fresh greens of a herbal collection. *Santolina chamaecyparissus* is a good hedging plant. It retains its leaves in winter and can be clipped into formal shapes for the herb or general garden. It is important to clip it only in late spring or early summer before the plant flowers and not in the fall. This is a perennial shrub, but not completely hardy; you may have to protect it with straw or sacking in winter. Alternatively, choose one of the evergreen forms, which are not quite as vigorous but very attractive, with dark green feathery foliage and bright button flowers. Santolina can be propagated from cuttings taken in the summer and planted out in their final position the following spring. *Santolina virens*, sometimes also known as *S. rosmarinifolia*, has vivid green leaves and soon forms a dense shrub, ideal for clipping into a formal hedge around the herb garden. You can also let it grow into a shaggy dome for the contrast of its bright yellow flowers against the green foliage. 'Primrose Gem' has pale yellow button flowers.

Insect deterrent

Cotton lavender retains its pungent oily scent even when dried. This acts as an insect deterrent and as a disinfectant. Traditionally, dried sprigs or branches were laid beneath rugs and carpets or hung amongst clothes in closets to repel the moths.

Strongly scented Santolina chamaecyparissus

Left: *A superb santolina and lavender hedge that takes full advantage of the similarities between these two aromatic hedging herbs, achieving a delightful contrast of color.*

Above: *Allowed to grow, Santolina virens, or holy flax, makes a bushy dome of feathery green foliage smothered in miniature yellow flowers, each on a tiny upright stem.*

1 To make a santolina hedge, position young plants about 12in(30cm) apart in light soil. Use alternate green and silver forms for a more decorative effect.

2 Choose similarly sized plants and firm them in well. The soil should come to the same level as it did in the original pot.

3 You might like to label the plants to remind you of the name of the variety you have chosen and the date you planted it.

Above: *Clipped before flowering, cotton lavender makes an excellent low hedge of dense silver-gray foliage. S. chamaecyparissus 'Nana', a dwarf form, is ideal for low edging.*

Santolina's striking silver foliage is the perfect foil for green and golden plants in the herb garden.

Growing sage as a vibrant foliage plant

Most people are familiar with sage as a pungent ingredient in sausages and stuffings, but it is also a valuable garden plant with many attractive varieties. Like so many of the more aromatic herbs, sage grows wild along the Mediterranean coast and makes a shrubby plant with soft, gray-green leaves. Growing to around 24in(60cm) high, the soft feltlike foliage makes a good contrast to smaller or glossier forms, either in the herb garden or in general herbaceous borders. The spike of flowers, which usually appears in midsummer in the plant's second year, is blue, purple, pink or white and attractive to bees. Garden varieties include many beautifully colored types that are useful for coordinating and contrasting in planned planting schemes. Trimming plants back after flowering prevents them becoming leggy and unattractive and encourages good busy growth, which is particularly important if you are growing them in tubs or containers. Sages thrive in a well-drained, preferably limey, soil and plenty of sunshine. You can sow seeds in spring, but propagating by cuttings or layering is more reliable for most varieties to come true to type. Plant out established cuttings 20in(50cm) apart. Dried leaves keep their flavor well and should be collected as the flower buds begin to open. Use them sparingly with heavy, fatty food, such as pork and goose. Sage is also prized for its medicinal qualities and may be taken as a tea for headaches, a gargle for sore throats or as an aid to digestion.

Above: Trim back stems before they get leggy to produce a dense growth of foliage about 24in(60cm) high. This giant sage contrasts with other foliage shapes and colors.

When dried, the leaves remain aromatic.

Right: The wonderful array of foliage types includes creams and purples, as well as the soft 'sage green'. Variegated forms are particularly decorative.

Garden sage (Salvia officinalis) *makes a shrubby plant with soft gray-green leaves.*

S. officinalis 'tricolor' *has attractive cream-bordered leaves washed with strawberry pink.*

Red or purple sage (S. officinalis 'purpurascens') *has attractive dark foliage.*

A rich flavor

Sage has a strong flavor, ideal for rich dishes. Combined with onion, it makes a stuffing for roast meats. The Italians use it to cut the richness of calves' liver sautéed in butter; in kebabs it is threaded between chunks of lamb. Vermont sage and sage Derby cheeses are strongly flavored and bright green. Use sage in small quantities with vegetable dishes.

S. officinalis can reach a height of 12-30in(30-75cm). It keeps its flavor well when dried and leaves are best collected for this purpose in spring.

Use sage fresh or dried. When fresh, chop or tear the leaves into smaller pieces.

The midsummer flower spikes of garden sage (Salvia officinalis).

Golden sage has softly smudged green and yellow leaves.

Salvia officinalis 'rosea' has pretty pink flowers.

Attractive clary sage (Salvia sclarea) is mostly decorative.

Lavender as a garden feature

Bees buzzing around the erect purple stems of a spiky lavender bush are the very image of the ideal country garden. In fact, *Lavandula angustifolia* grows wild all along the Mediterranean, where the soil is dry and stony and the climate sunny but exposed. This is an excellent plant for the bed or border, where it makes a long-lived shrubby bush about 39in(1m) high. The evergreen foliage is long and narrow, gray-green and glistening with aromatic oils. The densely flowered spikes that appear in summer are purple, although there are lighter and even white forms. With its gnarled woody stems and compact habit, lavender can be grown effectively as an attractive and fragrant hedge. Choose one of the smaller varieties, such as the semi-dwarf type *Lavandula angustifolia* 'Hidcote', which grows to about 24in(60cm). For a miniature hedge to border a knot-design herb garden or small border, consider *L. nana alba*, a white-flowering dwarf form that grows to 6in(15cm) in a sheltered position. Lavender plants can be propagated in the spring or fall by rooting strong shoots of new growth about 6in(15cm) long. Transfer established plants to a well-drained, sunny position, preferably with a rather poor, stony or sandy soil. It is also a good idea to prune the bushes back a little after they have flowered to prevent them from growing thin and straggly.

One of the most popular semi-dwarf forms, L. angustifolia 'Hidcote'.

L. 'Royal Purple' is strongly scented.

Left: *Grow lavender near a seat or bench, where you can enjoy the sight and smell of the wonderful flower spikes at close quarters. It is the perfect companion for old roses, scented stocks, garden pinks, hyssop and thyme.*

L. 'Jean Davis' has tiny pale flowers.

L. Twickel Purple is strongly scented.

L. nana alba *is a lovely dwarf form with white flowers.*

An unusual and delicate pink form (L.a. 'Loddon Pink').

L. 'Munstead' produces a mass of beautiful, small blue flowers.

Lavandula spica, *or* L. vera, *is the hardy, old-fashioned English lavender.*

Lavender oils

Oil of lavender - distilled from both the flowers and stalks - has been used for centuries as a cure for ailments and a popular scent. Rubbed on the temples, it is said to relieve a headache; massaged into aching arm and leg muscles, it acts like a liniment. Lavender is also a good insect repellent. The name is from 'lavare', Latin: to wash.

The scented stems were once burnt like joss sticks. Dried flowers are ideal for potpourris and scented cushions, or they can be infused to make scent.

Above: *Pick lavender on a sunny morning after the dew has evaporated and as the buds are beginning to open. Leave the stems long when harvesting and drying; remove later if required.*

Comfrey as a compost crop

Russian comfrey is a large perennial plant with soft, hairy leaves, each one often as long as 30cm(12in). It prefers a rich, moist soil and a shady position. You often see it growing wild along riverbanks and in the hedgerows. It is not really suited to the smaller, more formal herb garden, but in early summer it makes a fine display in a larger one, with its stems of pink, purple or even white, bell-shaped flowers. Other variations abound. A species with cream-colored flowers called *Symphytum tuberosum* is frequently seen in northern areas of Europe and the USA. The wild, Caucasian, prickly comfrey has bright blue flowers. You can grow comfrey from seed, but propagating it by means of rooted offsets is more common, as every piece of this vigorous plant will grow into a new plant. Keeping the plants under control might be more of a problem than propagating new ones. However, there are some smaller varieties. Both roots and leaves are used medicinally, as they have good healing properties. The bruised leaves are frequently used as the main ingredient in a compress to be applied to sprains, bone injuries and bruises. It is known to help reduce swelling and encourage the healing process. This has given rise to one of comfrey's common names: knitbone. Since it is rich in minerals and grows prolifically, comfrey is a wonderful composting material and it is worth growing a few plants simply for mulching down if you have a spare corner. Comfrey leaves allowed to infuse in rainwater are also valuable as a liquid fertilizer for garden plants.

Right: You can cut the leaves, stalks and flowers of comfrey for use at any time during the active growing period. Comfrey grows rapidly and you can take several crops during the season.

1 To make a rich compost for the garden, layer comfrey leaves with other plant material. The many layers can include vegetable waste, but avoid adding perennial weeds and roots.

Once it is 3-4ft(90-120cm) high, cover the entire heap with a 6in (15cm) casing of soil or old compost to retain moisture and heat.

Grass cuttings

Comfrey leaves

Compost from an existing heap as a 'starter'

2 Adding a layer of grass cuttings to the compost will speed up the heating process generated by the decomposing organic material. This kills off most of the weeds.

3 A layer of rich compost and soil from the base of the old compost heap will contain lively worms and bacteria to break down woody organic matter more quickly.

How to make liquid manure

A few comfrey plants are worth growing in a corner of the garden simply for the purpose of making a powerful and nutritious liquid manure from the leaves. Infuse an armful of fresh comfrey leaves in a barrel or bin of rainwater for about four weeks and then, braving the breathtaking stench, use the liquid as a plant food. The decomposed leaves can also be used to enrich the compost heap or to fertilize your tomatoes.

Left: Large fresh comfrey leaves tucked under and around plants act as a natural mulch to retain soil moisture. As the leaves rot down, the soil will be improved and enriched.

4 Water the compost if the material seems rather dry. The compost is ready to use when the mixture becomes crumbly and dark brown and has a rich, earthy smell.

Companion plants

Hoverflies (left) are attracted to the vegetable garden by such herbs as fennel (shown below) and will attack aphids on nearby plants.

In the wild, you do not often see plants devastated by insect damage or demolished by armies of slugs and snails. Nature has its own balance of complementary plants and predators, which relies on a rich and varied but often crucial mixture of plants and wildlife. Here there is no monoculture - the kind of artificial environment we try and impose on our gardens. If you are interested in gardening as organically as possible, you should explore the possibilities of companion planting: the pairing of herbs and wild plants with your hybridized flowers and vegetables, which will ultimately enrich the precious soil and not deplete it in the way that chemical control of pests and disease does. Companion planting is believed to work through the scent of certain plants acting as a deterrent - which is why so many useful plants are herbal ones - and through exudations of the roots, which alter the nutrient and bacterial make-up of the soil. For it to work effectively, you must introduce a carefully thought-out system of mixed planting that does not have regular beds separated by paths, but considers both the needs of individual plants and their effect on the soil by rotating crops not yearly, but as each comes into season. Thus, you might see strawberries interspersed with leeks; cauliflowers with celeriac or beetroot and lettuce.

Pot marigolds (Calendula) - at bottom right - are excellent companion plants in the vegetable garden. Their large root system makes them useful for planting beneath tomatoes and for making a kind of living mulch to conserve moisture. The bright golden flowers are a bonus, not only adding a splash of color between the rows, but also helping to deter aphids from beans (left) and tomatoes.

Right: The pretty blue flowers of borage attract butterflies and bees. This makes it a good companion plant for fruits and vegetables, such as strawberries and zucchinis, helping to improve crop yields.

Cabbage white butterflies (above) are deterred from attacking cabbage leaves if there are sage plants (below) planted nearby.

Herbs as companion plants

Herbs are not only beautiful - they are useful garden plants. Every plant in the garden affects the plants around it. It may be just by the large leaves offering shade and protection to more delicate plants. Some herbs deter pests and many attract beneficial insects that are valuable pollinators or act as predators of common garden pests.

The most common plant combinations are:

Borage, thyme and hyssop	attract bees which improve crop yield in strawberries and other fruit.
Chamomile	has been found to repel insect attacks, thus improving crop yields.
Chives	have a reputation for preventing black spot on leaves and deterring aphids.
Dill and fennel	attract hoverflies, which then go to work on aphids.
Garlic	with its strong odor is thought to be beneficial to roses.
Mint	especially the Pennyroyals have been found to be good fly and midge repellents.
Rosemary and thyme	mask the scent of carrots, which deters the carrot fly.
Sage	repels the cabbage white butterfly.
Nasturtium	has an excellent and interesting reputation as a companion plant. It keeps pests away from the vegetable garden, partly owing to the way it attracts aphids away from them. Nasturtium has also been found to repel ants and whitefly. It provides good ground cover and young leaves and flowers are delicious in salads.
Pot marigold	is a good all-round and attractive companion plant in the vegetable garden. It grows freely, is self-seeding and deters nematodes in the soil.

Planting a bay tree

Most people think of bay as an attractive, shrubby evergreen bush or as a highly decorative standard tree sporting a pompon of glossy green leaves on top of a single slender stem. The leaves are the main attraction, being large, shiny, deep green and highly aromatic. They can be picked and used at any time, but dry well too, the flavor actually strengthening and becoming more mellow. They are used extensively in cooking - in bouquet garnis, stocks, stews and marinades. Native to the Mediterranean, this handsome laurel is susceptible to frosts, so may even need protection in warm climates. In cooler ones, it is a good idea to plant the bay in a tub for overwintering in the greenhouse or conservatory. It does not grow well from seed so is usually propagated from cuttings, best taken in early summer. Bay prefers a light, well-drained soil, but grows slowly even in sunny, sheltered conditions. This makes it expensive to buy as a mature plant, but an excellent herb for trimming and clipping into formal shapes.

1 *Good drainage is essential, so add a few crocks in the bottom of the pot - it is worth saving any pieces of broken plant pot for this purpose.*

2 *Start filling the container with a light, sterilized soil. Synthetic particles are available to improve drainage. Make sure that the pot has been scrubbed and sterilized, too.*

3 *Take the bay out of its pot and lower it gently into the new container, holding the stem gently between your fingers and supporting the foliage against your hand.*

Make sure that the bay is planted at the same depth as it was in its original container.

4 When the plant is in place, continue filling the pot with more of the soil, taking care that the bay remains upright and in the correct position. Try to avoid getting any soil on the foliage.

Do not fill the pot right to the rim, but leave some space at the top to allow for watering

6 Stand the finished pot in a sunny, well-sheltered spot and bring it under cover at the first signs of frost. Bay produces small yellow-green flowers in late spring or early summer, followed by black berries.

5 A layer of small stones or gravel on the surface of the soil not only helps to retain moisture, but also looks attractive. In addition, it discourages weed growth.

Bay looks particularly good in a Mediterranean-style terracotta container.

Trimming and shaping a bay tree

1 A young, newly planted bay tree in a container has little shape to begin with. Light trimming will be necessary to provide the first outline of its future shape.

Once planted, the bay tree, *Laurus nobilis*, is easy to care for and can attain a mature height of 13-15ft(4-5m), even if it is growing in deep shade. Water it every day during the growing season, especially in hot weather. In winter, when the plant has been brought inside to escape the risk of frost damage and growth is slow, it will only require watering if the soil feels really dry. If the bay is growing in a container, feed it every week with a nitrogen feed from spring until the end of the summer to encourage healthy new leaves. Bay trees in pots can look particularly attractive when trained and shaped to grow into pyramids, balls and other topiary shapes. It is a useful way of removing leaves required for the kitchen and you can dry surplus leaves. Bay is slow to propagate; it may take up to six months for 6in(15cm) semi-ripe basal cuttings taken in late summer to root in a propagator with a soil heat of 55-60°F(13-15°C). It is possible to strike cuttings in a cold frame, but you will need endless patience as roots may not form for a year. To take a basal cutting, use a sharp knife to cut through the slight swelling at the base of a young shoot, just where it joins the main stem. The leaves of green bay may be smooth or crinkly at the edges. Other forms of bay include *L. n.* 'Aurea', with bright gold leaves in spring and *L. n.* 'Angustifolia', the willow leaf bay.

3 Tie horticultural string firmly to the stake, loop the ends around the main stem of the bay and tie the string, leaving space for growth.

Repot into a larger container after about a year or when the roots are visibly filling the soil. Place small containers on a deep saucer to provide extra moisture in really hot weather.

2 Insert a stake in the center of the pot, taking care not to damage the roots. Choose a firm, upright stake, as it will be used to train the main stem.

4 First decide on the shape that you would like to create. Start by trimming the long shoots to neaten the general appearance. This bay is too small to start removing branches from the main stem to form a standard.

5 As this is the first trim on a young bay, leave the sides and base wider than the top. Removing too many leaves at one time may slow growth.

6 Stand back and examine the shape from all sides between each cut. The aim is an even, rounded outline before you embark on the final trim.

7 Leave the stake in place until the main stem is firm enough to remain erect. If you remove uneven growth as it appears, the rounded shape will develop as the bush grows and slowly expands.

The leaves add a deep and lasting fragrance to potpourri, as well as being ideal for culinary use.

Creating topiary with box by pruning

Box is the traditional herb garden hedge plant; its tiny, tightly packed, evergreen leaves and insignificant flowers make it perfect for edgings, low hedges and geometric topiary shapes. It is often used to divide the formal herb garden into individual beds or geometric shapes or to create intricate, decorative knot gardens, where low hedges of box, rosemary or thyme are trained into elaborate patterns and mazes. Box is slow growing, but hardy enough to withstand all but the harshest climates. It will tolerate sun or semi-shade and any kind of soil except a bog. Encourage it to grow by cutting back the stems in late spring to about 12in(30cm). Box is best propagated from semi-ripe cuttings taken in summer and this is a good way of acquiring sufficient material to create hedging or edging. Established plants should be clipped or trimmed during the summer. Glossy green common box, *Buxus sempervirens*, is the variety most often seen; it is fully hardy, bushy and can grow to about 15ft (5m) in width as well as in height. However, there are variations, such as the small-leaved *B. microphylla* or the slow-growing Himalayan box, *B. wallichiana*, which has longer, narrower leaves.

2 Use another cane to mark the outer limits of your proposed shape - in this case a rounded dome. String or twine stretched between the stakes acts as a guideline for the curve.

Colored twine is easier to see when cutting.

1 Shaping a small-leaved, evergreen bush, such as box, is not a problem if you following these guidelines. First, position a central stake or cane to show the height and position of your shape.

3 Start clipping the straggly stems beyond your proposed shape with small shears or scissors. Stand back and check your progress occasionally.

4 Continue clipping the bulk of the bush, using the stakes or canes and twine as a guideline and remembering to maintain a three-dimensional shape as you work round the bush.

5 Once you have achieved your basic dome shape all round, use larger shears for the final trimming and a perfect finish. Leave the stakes in position for guidance.

6 The finished dome and other formal shapes, such as the pyramid shown above, provide the perfect leafy contrast to less formal garden plants and features. The dark green bulk adds weight and body to your scheme, too.

Herbs in a tub for the patio

Herbs look great in tubs: you can group them in large containers or grow them in individual pots on walls, patios, decks, balconies or terraces. They are also ideal for small garden areas: not only are they edible, they also produce a prolonged, attractive display and scent the area, too. Most patios tend to be sun traps, which suits many herbs very well, as they thrive in hot dry conditions. This does not mean you will not have to water them, as plants in pots dry out quickly, but once they have matured, even this job is minimal. Place a saucer underneath the container and pebbles or a mulch on the surface of the tub to keep it moist. If you are looking for the massed effect of several plants within a single container, choose carefully, so that they provide pleasing contrasts of shape, size and color, but are also compatible, enjoying the same kind of soil and climatic conditions. A range of heights will make the scheme more interesting, too; position the larger plants towards the rear - or in the center if the container is free standing. Pinch out the growing tips to encourage bushier, more compact plants. Try blending scents and flavors to create a tub designed to attract bees or butterflies, or plant a miniature bouquet garni garden; another scheme is a tub of herbs to complement barbecued meats.

1 If the pot has been used before, scrub it clean and sterilize it with a proprietary fluid. Put some crocks in the bottom of the container to keep the drainage hole free from soil.

2 Add a layer of washed small stones or gravel in the bottom of the tub for drainage. Tip the herbs gently out of their pots and stand them up straight in the tub.

4 Top up with a well-draining potting mixture. Sprinkle it in by hand to ensure it does not get on the leaves and that it fills all the spaces between the plants.

5 A sprinkling of small stones makes a neat finish and helps to reduce moisture loss until the plants mature.

Golden lemon thyme has tiny variegated foliage.

3 Add the rest of the herbs in the same careful manner, selecting each for its compatibility and a good contrast of type and color.

Tricolor sage (Salvia officinalis x tricolor)

Golden lemon thyme (T .v. citriodorus aureus)

6 The finished tub looks good immediately, with a fine variety of heights and foliage types. It will look even better after the plants have been growing for several weeks.

Thyme 'Archers Gold'

Curly gold marjoram (O. v. aureum crispum)

77

Creating a herb garden for the windowsill

A windowbox is the perfect way to grow a selection of culinary herbs in the minimum of space. The kitchen windowsill is an obvious site, providing the window opens conveniently enough for regular access to your mini garden. Make absolutely sure that the windowbox is firmly secured; use strong brackets or ties and check these periodically for wear or weathering. The box might be home-made from new or old timber, painted to match window frames or shutters; or it might be lightweight plastic, antique stone or terracotta. If the windows are too exposed a site, why not plant up an indoor windowbox, perfect for a few of the more tender species, such as basil. Regular cropping or trimming is important to ensure that the herbs remain small and leafy. Keep the box adequately watered and apply a liquid feed during the growing and cropping season. The soil soon runs out of essential nutrients in the confines of a box, especially where plants grow prolifically and where rain washes constantly through the soil. A mulch of small pebbles conserves moisture and reduces the effect of heavy rains.

1 Choose a selection of herbs - preferably with a variety of foliage shapes and textures - and stand them in the box or trough to see how they look together.

2 Take out the plants again and arrange a few crocks or broken pieces of pot in the bottom to prevent the potting mixture washing away.

3 Add 2-6in(5-15cm) of washed gravel or pea shingle to make a well-draining layer at the bottom of the box. Top up with planting mix.

78

4 Plant the herbs, keeping to your original plan and maintaining a balance of appearance, height and habit. Tip them gently out of their pots and into your hand, supporting the stem lightly between your fingers.

5 Top up with soil, making sure it settles between the plants without any air gaps. Do not fill right to the top of the box to allow for watering.

6 A sprinkling of gravel or small stones on top of the soil around the plants looks attractive and helps to slow down moisture loss.

Chives (Allium schoenoprasum)

Culinary thyme (Thymus vulgaris)

Sorrel (Rumex acetosa)

Sage (Salvia officinalis)

French tarragon (Artemisia dracunculus)

Parsley (Petroselinum crispum)

Oregano (Origanum vulgare)

7 The finished trough looks good and includes a useful blend of flavors for the cook. If you use plenty of herbs in cooking, reduce the number of plants in the box to two or three bigger plants.

Herbs in the kitchen

The flavor of fresh herbs is far more delicate than that of dried ones, so use them generously. Generally speaking, add them at the end of cooking for maximum effect. Mint, basil and tarragon change their flavor once dried, so do not expect them to taste the same as before. Add fresh, chopped herbs with a swirl of cream to home-made soups; sprinkle them on salads; tie them in tiny bundles to add to stocks and stews; or tuck sprigs of rosemary, sage or thyme under the roast joint with a slice of unpeeled onion and a clove of garlic to bring out the flavor.

79

A selection of herbs in containers

Lungwort
(Pulmonaria saccharata)

Golden feverfew,
(Tanacetum parthenium aureum)

Variegated comfrey
(Symphytum grandiflorum)

Golden sage
(Salvia icterina)

Broad leaf thyme
(T. pulegioides)

Purple-leaved violet
(Viola labradorica purpurea)

Rock hyssop
(Hyssopus aristatus)

Narrow leaf
golden marjoram
(Origanum
aureum var.)

Compact marjoram
(O. compactum)

Thyme 'Rainbow Falls'

Red houseleek
(Sempervivum
tectorum rubra)

Thymus drucei minus

Golden lemon thyme
(T. vulgaris citriodorus aureus)

Thyme
(T. vulgaris)

Parsley
(Petroselinum crispum)

French tarragon
(Artemisia dracunculus)

Mix and match

Choosing the right blend of herbs for your containers can be great fun. Even taking into account soil compatibility and whether the plants need sun or shade, there is plenty of scope to create pleasing contrasts of color, from darkest green to fresh lime; of foliage, from broadleaved to spiky or fleshy; and of size, from tall to tiny trailing varieties.

Sage
(Salvia officinalis)

Tricolor sage
(Salvia officinalis tricolor)

Lavender
(Lavandula spica 'Munstead')

Calamint
(Calamintha grandiflora)

Tricolor sage
(Salvia officinalis tricolor)

Artemisia
(Artemisia lanata pedamonta)

Thymus doerfleri
'Bressingham Pink'

Bugle (Ajuga reptans 'Burgundy Glow')

Thyme
(T. serpyllum rosea)

Thyme
(T. herba-barona)

81

Part Two

ENJOYING HERBS IN THE HOME

Herbs were once essential in the home: for cooking, for medicinal purposes and for every household use, from polishes and disinfectants to beauty products. Most were grown in the garden and those that were rarer or difficult to grow could be bought from a registered herbalist or apothecary. Today, the local supermarket supplies most of our needs - even fresh herbs for cooking. Yet our enthusiasm for growing herbs in our own gardens, patios and even windowboxes is growing, as they fit today's busy lifestyles perfectly, too. Herb plants mature quickly, producing almost instant effects. They are highly decorative, offering a vast choice of flower and foliage color, shape and form; yet their effect is subtle, perfect for modern complementary color schemes and relaxing areas. Best of all, they are wonderfully scented and edible, too, which makes them truly 'garden worthy'. Herbs can mingle with herbaceous and bedding plants or be used to create a complex herb garden of different fragrances and flavors; they adapt well to a modern or traditional themes, to formal and informal specifications and are ideal for growing in containers. By all means exploit their potential as decorative plants, but it would be a shame not to pinch off a few sprigs here and there for the kitchen or experiment with some of herbs' other uses explored on these pages.

Left: A stunning display of fresh and dried herbs.   *Right: Sweet cicely leaves decorate a cake.*

Freezing herbs

We are so familiar with the idea of drying herbs to preserve them that we often forget that most of them can be stored very successfully in the freezer. In fact, for some herbs, such as parsley, basil and tarragon, freezing is by far the best option, as their flavor changes quite dramatically when they are dried. Frozen herbs can be chopped and added to soups, stews, marinades, sauces - in fact to any dish - but they cannot be used as a garnish. Pick the herbs fresh and sort them out to remove any dead or withered parts. Then arrange them in sprigs. You need not blanch them, but give them a quick rinse in cold water and dry them on kitchen paper or a clean tea towel to remove any small insects. Freeze them in small quantities, making sure the bags are well labeled. For convenience, you may like to put together some useful combinations, such as a bouquet garni mix or, say, parsley, chives and tarragon for adding to egg or fish dishes. To use the herbs, chop them in their frozen state as soon as you remove them from the freezer. Instead of freezing herbal mixtures in sprigs, you could chop them finely together and freeze them in ice cubes to pop into stews and sauces. Herb flowers, such as borage, can be frozen in the same way for adding to drinks.

2 Combine the chopped herbs and sprinkle a little of the mixture into each compartment of the ice cube tray. You may need extra trays if you are freezing large quantities.

Marjoram

Thyme

Parsley

Sage

1 Herb mixtures frozen in ice cube trays are so convenient for adding to stews, soups and sauces at any time of year. First chop the herbs finely with a sharp knife or herb mill.

Herb flowers in ice

Some herb flowers, such as borage and salad burnet, are traditionally added to summer drinks. Freeze the flowers in filtered or bottled water; chemically treated tapwater tends to go cloudy when frozen.

3 Top up the container, ideally with filtered or bottled water, and place the tray in the freezer. The herb cubes will remain usable for several months.

Freezing individual fresh herbs

Freeze individual herbs in small sprigs. When you are ready to use them, shred them off the stem while they are still frozen.

1 Gather the herbs and lightly wash the trimmed sprigs in clean water to remove any dirt or small insects.

2 Absorb any excess moisture by patting the sprigs gently with a piece of kitchen paper or a clean tea towel.

3 Package the herbs ready for freezing in individual plastic bags. Squeeze out as much air as possible, fasten and label clearly.

Drying herbs

Although it is possible to grow a few of the more compact herb varieties in pots on the windowsill to carry you through the winter, this will rarely keep pace with demand if you are a keen herb user. Drying your own herbs enables you to continue using them all year. However, some herbs are simply not worth drying; evergreens, such as thyme, for example, should be fine for cropping right through the winter, while parsley, chervil and fennel simply do not dry well, losing all their flavor in the process. Drying herbs is quite simple. When you have harvested and sorted them, just tie them in bunches and hang them in any shady but warm and well-ventilated place, such as an attic or shed. The quicker the herbs are dried, the better the color and flavor and the less chance there will be of them going musty. Some people use a well-ventilated airing cupboard successfully or dry herbs in a cool oven with the door ajar. Another traditional method is to use a drying cupboard, where the herbs are set out on meshed trays. This is a useful strategy for flowerheads. It is also possible to buy an electrical version for quicker and more predictable results. Once the herbs are dried, strip the leaves from the stems and store them in airtight containers. To dry seeds, collect the seedheads just before they ripen and dry them in bunches upside down with a cloth or paper below to catch any seeds that fall. Strip the rest of the seedheads from the stalk and leave them to dry out completely for another week or so before storing.

Lemon balm

Rosemary

Santolina

1 *Gather your chosen herbs for drying and lay the sprigs or branches all facing the same way. Tie the stalks together loosely into small bunches with string, twine or cotton.*

2 *Hang the bunches to dry in a warm, airy place away from direct sunlight. A barn or attic is ideal. The bunches should hang freely or they will take too long to dry and become dusty.*

Santolina

Rosemary

Lemon balm

3 *When the herbs are dry, shred them off the stalks, taking care not to crumble them too much or they will not retain so much flavor. Some leaves, such as bay, can be stored whole.*

4 *Store the dried herbs in glass or ceramic jars with tight-fitting lids. Label them clearly and keep them away from direct light. Replace dried herbs every twelve months.*

Dried herbs around the home

Dried herbs are useful when fresh ones are not available, particularly those that do dry successfully, such as rosemary, sage, thyme, mint and lemon balm. Some, such as fennel, dill, cumin and coriander, are better when the seeds are dried and stored. Remember that dried herbs have a more intense flavor than fresh ones, so you will only need a pinch or a teaspoonful, rather than a bunch of leaves. Dried herbs also make refreshing herbal teas and household products, such as mothbags and small scented bags. Scented dried herbs include lavender, clove carnation, roses, santolina, scented pelargoniums, bergamot and woodruff.

Making a potpourri

Long before air fresheners, pots or bowls of fragrant or spicy leaves and flowers were used to scent and sweeten the home. The name potpourri comes from the French meaning literally 'rotten pot', as the earliest types were made by packing petals down into a sealed jar until they rotted to make a highly fragrant thick paste or wad. The old potpourri jars were made of china with a lid to cover the mixture until it was warmed and the scents released. Today, a potpourri is more likely to be made by the dry method, which involves assembling and thoroughly drying a good blend of aromatic herbs and spices. Color and shape are equally important to produce an attractive mixture for displaying in bowls or jars. Rose petals are usually the main ingredient. Gather young petals on a dry day after the dew has lifted. A few rosebuds are worth drying, too, for their decorative effect in the finished mixture. Dry these as quickly as possible, using wire trays for better air circulation. It is important that all the potpourri material is thoroughly dried to avoid any risk of mildew. Add rosemary, thyme, lavender, clove carnation, lemon balm or any of the sweet or spicy herbs to your roses, plus a few ground spices, such as cinnamon, cloves and ginger. A little powdered orris root helps to preserve the fragrance for many years.

4 Start mixing dried flowers, leaves, including barberry, bay or lemon verbena and, say, calendula petals. Sweet herbs might be marjoram or peppermint. Store each one in an airtight tub before mixing.

Calendula Bay leaves Rosebuds Dried seedpods

Peony petals Assorted flowerheads Larkspur

Dried seedpods Rosebuds Rose petals

1 You will need a large wooden, glass or ceramic bowl with a wide neck for mixing and stirring the dried ingredients with a spoon. Rub a few drops of clove oil into your hands.

2 Rub the bowl with the aromatic oil until it is smeared all round. Other suitable essential oils include geranium, rosemary, lavender or, for a fruity potpourri, orange or tangerine.

3 A typical potpourri mixture might consist of roughly 4 parts rose petals to 1 part mixed scented flowers, 1 part aromatic leaves, ¼ part calendula petals and ½ part sweet herb.

5 *Grind up an assortment of spices such as those shown here and add to the mixture with a fixative, such as myrrh, orris root, gum benzoin or dried tonquin beanpods.*

Coriander

Nutmeg

Mace

Dried ginger root

Orris root

Allspice

Ground ginger

Cinnamon

Cloves

6 *Stir all the ingredients together to create an interesting blend of shapes, types, colors and scents, using different petals, leaves and seedheads.*

Adjust the blend if necessary by adding new ingredients.

7 *Add a few drops of rosemary, basil or lavender oil and give a good final stir, checking that the scent is spicy, flowery or fruity enough.*

8 *Spoon the finished potpourri into a jar with a tight stopper and leave it for about six weeks to develop and mature. Stir it every few days with a wooden spoon.*

9 *Decant the potpourri into a bowl or into a container with perforations that allow the aroma to escape. You can buy revival oils if the scent begins to fade after about a year.*

1 *Melt 12oz(340gm) of beeswax with 3.5 pints(1.75liters) of turpentine in the top of a double saucepan with boiling water below. Take extra care, as the turpentine is inflammable.*

2 *In a separate saucepan, bring 2 pints(1 liter) of water to the boil. Stir in 2oz(60gm) of soft soap until it has dissolved completely. Soft soap is sold for washing delicate fabrics.*

Household uses

Many of the more pungent herbs can be effective at deterring insects around the home. Leaves, seeds or stems can be dried, chopped and packed into muslin bags; you can hang sprigs of herbs in a suitable place, such as a wardrobe or simply place the live herb on a convenient windowsill or table. Equal quantities of dried rosemary, sage and mint stitched into muslin bags are said to deter moths. Alternatively, hang sprigs of thyme to dry among your clothes hangers. Sprigs of mint, on the other hand, are supposed to repel flies, so hang this in large bunches in the kitchen. The aromatic scent from a pot of basil also deters houseflies, while a couple of cloves of garlic in a small pot near your houseplants may keep aphids at bay. Why not sprinkle your freshly laundered linen with a strong infusion of fragrant herbs, such as eau de cologne mint or sweet marjoram, like the sixteenth-century housewife? Or if you have antique or fine furniture you may like to try your hand at making your own furniture polish: beeswax, turpentine and soap are combined over a low heat then scented with essential oils, such as lavender or rosemary.

3 *When both mixtures have cooled down, gradually stir the soap solution into the softened beeswax and beat gently until it takes on the appearance of thick cream.*

Take the pan away from the stove to help the mixture cool more quickly.

4 *Add a few drops of essential herb oil, such as lavender or rosemary. Do not to add too much or the scent will be overpowering.*

5 Pour the polish into a suitable jar while still softened and allow it to set. Enquire locally to find a stockist of jars and labels - try beekeeping suppliers.

Making moth bags

Combine the following dried herbs and place a spoonful of the mixture onto a square of fabric with a little stuffing to give it shape and bulk: 4 parts mint; 4 parts rue; 2 parts southernwood; 2 parts rosemary; 1 part ground cloves. Bring the edges of the fabric together and tie to make a 'dolly bag' or stitch the herbs into muslin or cotton bags.

Glass jar with screw-top lid.

Use scraps of cotton fabric to make moth repellent bags.

6 Making your own household polishes and mothbags will scent your home with the sweet smell of herbs. They also make good gifts.

Rue

Rosemary

Southernwood

1 Fill a herbal sachet with your favorite herb or a suitable mixture. The spicy combination featured here is said to ease headaches. Stitch or glue the sachet ready to put inside your pillow.

Lemon balm

Marjoram

Lavender

Cloves

2 Cut two pieces of fabric into a square or rectangle. With the right sides together, pin or tack around three sides. Sew securely.

Making a herbal pillow

Dried herbs have probably always been used among the bedding, if not to encourage sweet dreams then perhaps to deter the bed bugs. Straw in the mattress had its own pleasant fragrance, but woodruff, dried lavender or rose petals were sometimes added to clear the mind and encourage restful sleep. Dried hops were a particular favorite, as they have a definite soporific effect; you can still buy hop pillows today, recommended for poor sleepers and insomniacs. You may also see small herbal pillows scented with a particular herb, such as lavender, lemon balm or rosemary, or a mixture of herbs and spices similar to potpourri blends. However, these are quite easy to make up yourself, using your favorite fragrances or a particular mixture suited to your mood; an anti-stress pillow, a headache pillow, and so on. Stitch the herbs into a muslin bag to slip inside your pillowcase or include them in a small stuffed fabric pillow, perhaps made up from a remnant of material to match your bedroom curtains or your bedlinen. Alternatively, you could make a small, decorative, herbal pillow in the Victorian style, by edging it with lace or frills and dressing it up with embroidery, applique or beadwork. Another idea is to pad a plain wooden clothes hanger with cotton wadding and a small herbal sachet. All the items shown on these pages make excellent presents.

3 Turn the pillowcase right side out, making sure the corners are fully extended by pushing them out firmly. Begin stuffing the pillow quite tightly, using clean stuffing material.

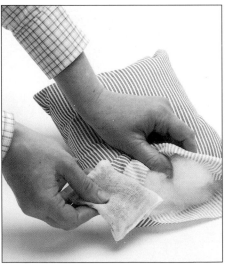

4 Before the pillowcase is fully stuffed, slip in the herbal sachet. Bury the sachet completely in the stuffing to avoid feeling the prickly dried herbs through the pillow.

6 Decorate the pillows with lace or frills or leave plain. Slip one in your pillowcase at night or cradle it by your head to relieve stress, depression or a headache, depending on the herbs within.

5 Fold under the remaining raw edges and pin or tack the two sides together. Slip stitch by hand or sew all round the pillow to make a border.

Herbal toys and novelties

Adding a few herbs to simple toys makes them all the more enjoyable to handle, especially the tactile 'bean bag' novelties. Use dried herbs known for their cheering effect, such as mint, rosemary or basil. Or sprinkle a little catnip, *Nepeta*, inside a simple stuffed mouse to drive your cat into a frenzy of excitement.

1 Make a template by drawing a frog shape on a piece of card. Cut it out and pin it onto a double thickness of fabric folded right sides together before cutting.

2 With right sides together, remove the template and pin the pieces, leaving the tail open for stuffing. Hand sew or machine stitch.

3 Turn the frog the right way out, fully extending the head and legs. Loosely fill with dried peas and a teaspoonful of herbs.

Dried mint   Split peas

4 When filled, stitch up the tail and the frog is ready to strike a pose, be used for juggling or as an antidote to stress.

Making beauty products

Natural products are popular again for the face and body, reviving recipes that were probably in use hundreds of years ago. Virtually all beauty preparations can include herbs in some form, either chopped fresh or dried, steeped in oil, infused in water or distilled to a fine essence. If not used for their scent, they may be valued for their soothing or astringent properties. Bath bags are easily made: simply tie up a handful of dried or fresh herbs in a piece of muslin and suspend this beneath the hot tap when filling the bath. Try a mixture of valerian, chamomile and meadowsweet to relax; rosemary or mint to stimulate. An infusion of one of the astringent herbs, such as elderflower, fennel or yarrow, makes a fine face tonic; to moisturize, mix three parts rosewater with four parts glycerine and add three parts of your favorite herb made up into a strong infusion - comfrey for its healing properties, perhaps, or soothing chamomile. For the hair, add a strong infusion of herbs to unscented baby shampoo; rosemary or sage to bring a shine to dark hair; chamomile or marigold to highlight blonde. You might even try your hand at making your own Elizabethan washball by grating down a couple of bars of glycerine soap, and melting them over a pan of hot water with a tablespoon of fine oatmeal, a few drops of essential herbal oil and 1oz(30gm) of your favorite chopped herbs. Pour into a mold lined with wax paper.

1 Comfrey has soothing, healing properties that make it an excellent cream for delicate skin. Shred about 2oz(60gm) of dried or 4oz(115gm) of fresh leaves into a heatproof bowl.

2 Pour ⅓ to ⅔ pint (150-300ml) boiling water onto the leaves to produce the strong infusion required for making toiletries.

3 Leave the herbs to steep for at least 15 minutes, but preferably 2-3 hours to make a strong infusion. Never use an aluminum container.

4 Pour ⅓ pint (150ml) of good-quality oil - preferably an olive or almond oil - into the top of a double boiler. Have ready some beeswax and cocoa butter.

5 Break about two tablespoons of beeswax into the top of the double boiler containing the oil and allow it melt slowly over the boiling water below.

6 Now add approximately two tablespoons of cocoa butter to the pan and allow it to melt. The ingredients described here are available from most drugstores.

7 Strain ⅓ pint (150ml) of the infusion into a pan and warm it without boiling. Use stainless steel, ceramic, glass or enamel pans.

8 Add a teaspoon of borax to the warmed infusion and stir until dissolved. Keep chemicals away from the eyes and skin.

9 Add 2 teaspoons of good-quality honey to the pan and stir until well-dissolved. Inferior honey gives a less pleasant result.

10 Remove both pans from the heat and slowly add the infusion/borax/honey mixture to the oil/wax one. Stir carefully to blend the contents together a little.

13 Making your own beauty products is not only simple and fun, but all those natural ingredients are good for your skin, too.

Elderflower toner - a strong infusion of elderflowers.

Comfrey cream - good for the face and children's skin.

12 Pot up the cream into suitable jars with screw-top lids. Label all pots, bottles and cosmetic jars clearly so that you know what is in them.

11 Beat the infusion into the wax mixture until it goes thick and creamy - this will happen as it starts to cool. Use a wooden spoon or electric whisk.

Chamomile cleansing milk - steep flowers in milk for 3 hours. Refrigerate.

Making a pomander

Pomanders take their name from the French 'pomme d'ambre', or amber apple, a reference to the ambergris that together with rosewater, flower petals and other scented ingredients, was mixed and rolled between oiled hands into small balls. When dried, they were made into necklaces and bracelets. These aromatic accessories were popular in the 15th and 16th centuries, when they were thought to ward off the plague and also masked many of the unpleasant odors of the day. You can make your own scented jewelry by pounding fresh rose petals - preferably one of the old fashioned scented varieties - to a paste and shaping them into beads with a complementary essential herb oil, such as geranium, rosemary or rose. Dry the beads on a tray covered with waxed paper on a sunny windowsill or in the airing cupboard and pierce them with a hot needle before they become completely hard. Later on, pomanders were made of precious metal, decorated porcelain or even wood and filled with fragrant spices, sometimes mixed with earth. Priests and doctors who tended plague victims carried a simple orange, lemon or lime stuck with cloves and rolled in spices. A pomander such as this is easy to make and will keep your clothes smelling sweet for years in the wardrobe or in a drawer.

3 Roll the pomander in a mixture of ground spices and orris root to preserve its spicy flavor. Take good care not to dislodge any of the cloves.

Orris root

Ginger

Nutmeg

Cinnamon

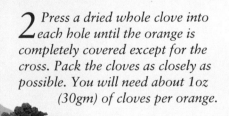

1 Prick an orange all over, using a knitting needle to make the holes. Leave a central cross for fastening the ribbon - see photograph at far right.

2 Press a dried whole clove into each hole until the orange is completely covered except for the cross. Pack the cloves as closely as possible. You will need about 1oz (30gm) of cloves per orange.

4 Tie the pomander with a length of satin or velvet ribbon to cover the cross - green, red or purple look the most traditional; or choose something to match a particular color scheme.

5 Place the finished pomander carefully in a brown paper bag - never a plastic one - and leave it in the airing cupboard or a dark, well-aired cupboard until it has shrunk and hardened. Hang it in the wardrobe to scent your clothes or bedlinen.

As an alternative, you could try using a lemon or a lime instead of an orange to make the pomander.

Making a tussie-mussie

Tussie-mussies are handheld posies. In the 16th century, they were made up of the most aromatic and/or antiseptic flowers and herbs and, like the pomander, they could be carried about the streets and held politely up to the nose as protection from disease or when the surrounding stench threatened to become too overpowering. These posies were as pretty as they were practical, and later on people began to give them as presents, as a token of endearment or to mark a special occasion, such as a birth or marriage. Very often, the herbal and floral components had a special meaning of their own according to the 'language of flowers' (thus, rosemary signified remembrance, lemon balm meant sympathy, bay represented nobility, and so on). It is easy to make your own tussie-mussie, choosing the individual ingredients carefully for color and shape, as well as meaning. Start with a central flower and work your way outwards in a circular design, binding the stems with florists' tape to keep the posy as tight as possible. The final layer should be made up of large leaves. Some people like to place a frilled doily behind to set the whole thing off. You can dry a tussie-mussie and keep it forever by hanging it in a dry, dark place.

Jellies and preserves

1 Roughly chop 4lb(about 2kg) of cooking apples or crab apples; you need not remove the core, pips or skin.

One of the most useful and delicious ways to preserve herbs is to make them up into jams, jellies, vinegars and pickles. A good apple jelly is easily scented with a sprig of your favorite herb and then used as an accompaniment to roast meats - rosemary jelly with lamb, sage jelly with pork, etc., or as a sauce with desserts, such as ice cream. Save some of your most scented (unsprayed) rose petals for rose petal jam or use half roses, half strawberries for pretty summer sponge cakes. A tasty herb-flavored vinegar is equally simple to make: simply add a bunch of your chosen herb to a good-quality wine or cider vinegar and keep it in a well-sealed glass bottle for two to three weeks. Strain off the herbs when you are satisfied the flavor is strong enough, then pour it into clean, dry bottles. Dill, mint and tarragon are popular vinegar herbs for salad dressings, marinades or mayonnaise. Herbs and spices perk up vegetable pickles and chutneys: add a bunch of parsley, tarragon, thyme, basil, marjoram or savory to your favorite recipe. Home-made candies are really special; angelica stems or sweet cicely roots are the best. Any attractive herb flowers or leaves can be crystallized and used to decorate cakes and desserts, providing they are dry and in good condition. Dip each one in whisked egg white and then in sugar before drying them slowly. Store them in an airtight tin.

2 Put the chopped apple in a large pan with a large sprig of your chosen herb - rosemary is the one being used here, ideal for lamb and game.

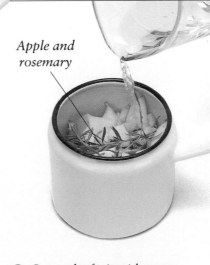

Apple and rosemary

3 Cover the fruit with water and bring the mixture to the boil. Then allow it to simmer gently. Do not cover the pan.

4 Stir the mixture occasionally with a wooden spoon. When the apples have softened to a pulp, remove the pan from the heat.

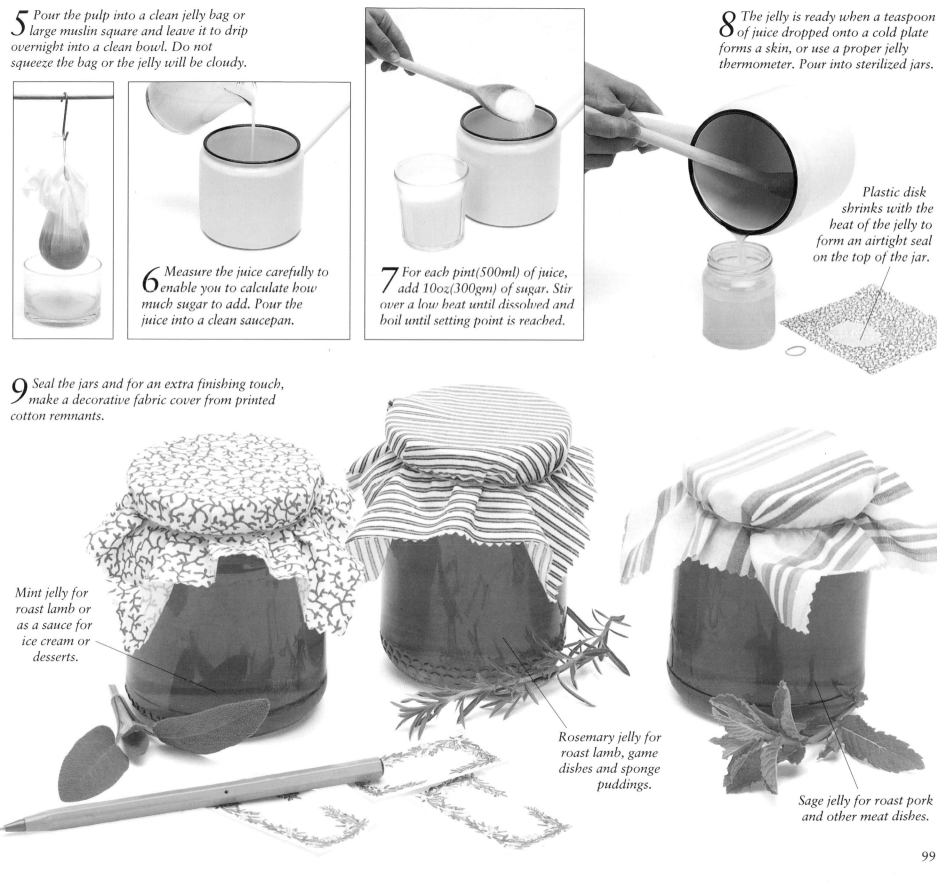

5 Pour the pulp into a clean jelly bag or large muslin square and leave it to drip overnight into a clean bowl. Do not squeeze the bag or the jelly will be cloudy.

6 Measure the juice carefully to enable you to calculate how much sugar to add. Pour the juice into a clean saucepan.

7 For each pint (500ml) of juice, add 10oz (300gm) of sugar. Stir over a low heat until dissolved and boil until setting point is reached.

8 The jelly is ready when a teaspoon of juice dropped onto a cold plate forms a skin, or use a proper jelly thermometer. Pour into sterilized jars.

Plastic disk shrinks with the heat of the jelly to form an airtight seal on the top of the jar.

9 Seal the jars and for an extra finishing touch, make a decorative fabric cover from printed cotton remnants.

Mint jelly for roast lamb or as a sauce for ice cream or desserts.

Rosemary jelly for roast lamb, game dishes and sponge puddings.

Sage jelly for roast pork and other meat dishes.

Making herb oils and butters

Another way to preserve your favorite culinary herb is to use it to flavor vinegars and oils for cooking or in marinades, salad dressings and sauces. Basil, thyme, tarragon, dill, fennel or even crushed garlic are all suitable. When making a herb vinegar, use a good-quality, mild-flavored vinegar, otherwise it will swamp the delicate flavor of the herbs. Fill a glass jar or bottle with vinegar and steep the herbs in it for about three weeks, making sure it is tightly stoppered to prevent evaporation. Avoid bottles with metal caps, as these react with the vinegar and go black. Herb oils are made in a similar way, but need regular stirring to help the flavor develop. Keep them in a warm position, but not too warm, otherwise the oil will cook and spoil. Herb butters are another way to enjoy fresh herbs out of season. Soften the butter and beat in a selection of chervil, parsley, watercress, tarragon, mint or lemon thyme with garlic, lemon juice and seasoning. Shape the butter in small pats and freeze. To use, melt a pat over grilled steak, fish, vegetables or garlic bread.

4 *Fasten a piece of clean muslin over the mouth of the jar and place it on a sunny windowsill or similar warm place in the kitchen.*

5 *Shake or stir the oil with a wooden spoon once a day for about two weeks. The oil may absorb some of the color of the herb.*

1 *Using a pestle and mortar, lightly bruise a handful of your chosen herb - in this case it is basil.*

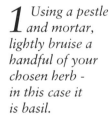

2 *Loosely fill a clean, but not necessarily sterilized, glass jar or wide-mouthed bottle with the bruised herbs.*

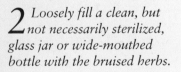

3 *Cover the herbs with a good-quality, mild-tasting oil, such as sunflower, safflower or a mild olive oil. You could use tarragon, thyme or rosemary instead.*

6 When the oil has absorbed the flavor of the oil, strain it through muslin into a suitable container.

7 Press the herbs to extract oil and flavor. Repeat the entire process with fresh herbs for extra strength.

8 Herbal oil can take its place in the kitchen amongst other herbal preserves. Making oils, vinegars and butters is a great way to preserve the true flavor of many of the more elusive herbs, such as basil and tarragon.

Tarragon vinegar

Basil oil

Pickled onions made with herb spiced vinegar.

Chervil, parsley, shallots and garlic for making herb butter.

Herb butters can be shaped and frozen for adding to vegetables, steaks and grills. Blanch a large handful each of watercress, parsley and chervil for 30 seconds in boiling water and then blend or pound them with one chopped shallot, a clove of garlic and a pinch of salt. Beat or blend the mixture into 8oz(225gm) of butter.

Making herb teas for all occasions

More and more people are switching to herbal teas, or tisanes, as they are sometimes called. Not only are they caffeine-free, but there is a whole range of plain and blended flavors to choose from, some to be drunk merely for pleasure, others as a remedy for sleeplessness, stress or headaches. You need not buy expensively packaged herb teas in bags when your own herbs, fresh or dried, are equally effective. If you do not find it quite to your taste, you can sweeten your herb tea with sugar, but honey is better, preferably a mild-flavored honey. Try experimenting with different flavors of honey to complement a particular herb - lime blossom honey is superb taken with a lime flower tea, for example.

You can make herbal teas in the same way as other types of tea; pour one pint of boiling water over ½oz(15gm) of dried herb or about 1oz(30gm) of fresh herb and leave the mixture to infuse for about ten minutes before straining it, depending on how strong you like your tea - some of the stronger flavors, such as chamomile and rosemary may only need the briefest dip. Others, including fennel and rosehip, need time to develop and yet will not get bitter as they infuse. You can make them in a kitchen jug or a proper decorative teapot; herb teas look particularly attractive when served in the transparent type of pot. Some pots are designed with a removable central compartment for tea leaves or herbs, which usefully keeps them in place. Alternatively, use a strainer when you pour out the tea; the small bamboo type you sometimes see imported from China are ideal. Never use an aluminum container. If you are drinking herb tea purely for pleasure, then lime blossom, chamomile, fennel and peppermint are among the most popular. You can also buy blends of several herbs designed to be drunk at certain times, at breakfast, for example, before going to bed, and so on.

1 Melissa, or lemon balm, tea is very refreshing and is believed to have restorative powers. Shred a handful of fresh leaves into a suitable teapot.

2 Add boiling water to cover and allow to stand. Try to use bottled or filtered water when making herb teas to keep a good color and flavor with no scumminess.

Herbal remedies

A weak herb tea can be very soothing if you or your digestion are a little under the weather. Herbal remedies are best taken at the onset of a headache or a cold. Try three small glasses three times a day. Always consult your doctor if symptoms are persistent or more serious.
For headaches: *rosemary, lavender, ground ivy, betony.*
For insomnia: *chamomile, elderflower, lime blossom, fennel (seed), lemon verbena.*
For colds and fevers: *borage or sorrel leaves infused in boiling water to make a herb tea are said to bring down a fever. Try mint tea with lemon juice for a cold.*
For coughs: *borage, sage, anise and marsh mallow are soothing.*

1 *Chamomile tea is made in the same way: infuse fresh or dried flowerheads in boiling water within the inner compartment of the teapot. You can flavor the resulting tea with honey.*

2 *Pour the boiling water over the herb and leave it to infuse until the tea is strong enough for you.*

3 *Chamomile tea is a sedative and is said to prevent nightmares and relieve nausea. It is also used as a skin cleanser.*

3 *Delicious lemon balm tea can be drunk at any time, but is particularly effective when taken as a treatment for colds, headaches and fevers. Drink it or simply add some of the tea to your bathwater.*

Herbal drinks

Herbs can be used to make some delicious and unusual cold drinks. A chilled mint drink is wonderfully refreshing on a hot day or you could make a selection of cordials - elderflower, rosehip or spiced blackcurrant - to be diluted with hot or cold water, according to your fancy or the weather. To make traditional lemonade, add one thinly sliced lemon, a small piece of grated fresh ginger and a bunch of apple mint or lemon balm to 4pints(2 liters) of cold water. Bring to the boil and simmer for 30 minutes to reduce the liquid by half. Strain and stir in 4oz(110gm) of brown sugar until it has dissolved. Chill the lemonade before serving. For something a little stronger, try steeping sprigs of borage, rosemary, lemon balm, mint or woodruff with a teaspoon of white sugar in a bottle of white wine for about an hour ; chill, strain and serve. Alcoholic drinks have always depended on herbs and spices to add flavor: juniper berries lend a distinctive bitterness to gin, while vermouth, absinthe and chartreuse have a wonderful herbal bouquet. Ales and wines often include a selection of aromatic or bitter herbs, some to improve the taste, others as a preservative or for some medicinal effect. The earliest ales would have been strongly flavored with herbs, including rosemary, yarrow or ground ivy, which also acted as a preservative. Mead and metheglin - the very first alcoholic drinks - were made from honey, herbs and flowers.

1 *For a deliciously fresh, iced drink, take 4oz(100gm) of herbs, such as mint, lemon balm or lemon verbena, and pound them to a pulp using a pestle and mortar or food processor.*

Spearmint
Mentha spicata

2 *Add 1oz(30gm) of finely ground sugar and pound it together with the herbs until it forms a paste.*

3 *Boil 2 pints(1 liter) of water with 2oz (60gm) of finely ground sugar for five minutes. Cool the sugar syrup. Add the juice of two large lemons.*

4 *Now add the pulped herbs - in this case mint - to the cooled syrup mixture. You may notice that the herbs have darkened considerably in the meantime. This is quite normal.*

5 Stir the ingredients together thoroughly then cover the container and chill it for several hours before serving.

6 Transfer the drink to an attractive glass jug and decorate it with a sprig of mint or whichever herb is appropriate.

Elderflower cordial is made by combining an infusion of the flowers with a strong sugar syrup.

Other herb drinks

Aspi is made by steeping three tablespoons of lavender flowers in a bottle of white wine; add a little sugar syrup and half a glass of brandy. Lassi is a refreshing Indian drink made by whisking yogurt with chopped mint and spices. Sweeten it with sugar or, to accompany savory dishes, add salt to taste. For an aromatic liqueur, put 8oz(225gm) of scented flower petals, such as violets, in a large glass jar. Cover with a quart of vodka or rectified spirit, cover and leave for one month. Strain; add sugar to taste.

7 A selection of refreshing drinks for summer might include an iced mint drink, a herb-infused white wine and a flowery cordial to be diluted with still or carbonated water.

Iced mint drink

Spearmint

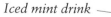

Aspi made with white wine and lavender flowers.

Index to Herbs

Credits

The majority of the photographs featured in this book have been taken by Neil Sutherland and are © Colour Library Books. The publishers wish to thank the following photographers for providing additional photographs, credited here by page number and position on the page, i.e. (B)Bottom, (T)Top, (C)Center, (BL)Bottom left, etc.

John Glover: 10, 16(BL), 17(B), 20(TR), 21(T), 22, 22-3(BC), 45(B), 46(BC), 57(TL), 64(BL), 68(BL, BR), 69(TC, B), 75(BL)

John Feltwell (Wildlife Matters): 68(T © Sheila Apps), 69(TL)

Acknowledgments

The publishers would like to thank Rosemary and David Titterington, Marian and everyone at Iden Croft Herbs for their help and patience during the photography sessions. Thanks are also due to Cadmore Lodge Hotel near Tenbury Wells, Worcestershire for providing space for photography.